AMERICA BETRAYED

AMERICA BETRAYED

How a Christian Monk Created America & Why the Left Is Determined to Destroy Her

DAVID HOROWITZ

FINAL
BATTLE
BOOKS

Final Battle Books may be purchased in bulk at special discounts for sales promotion, corporate gifts, fund-raising, or educational purposes. Special editions can also be created to specifications. For details, contact the Special Sales Department, Skyhorse Publishing, 307 West 36th Street, 11th Floor, New York, NY 10018 or info@skyhorsepublishing.com.

Final Battle Books® and Skyhorse Publishing® are registered trademarks of Skyhorse Publishing, Inc.®, a Delaware corporation.

Visit our website at www.skyhorsepublishing.com.
Please follow our publisher Tony Lyons on Instagram
@tonylyonsisuncertain

10 9 8 7 6 5 4 3 2 1

Library of Congress Cataloging-in-Publication Data is available on file.

Hardcover ISBN: 978-1-5107-8147-4
eBook ISBN: 978-1-5107-8148-1

Cover design by David Ter-Avanesyan
Cover image by Ty Fritz

Printed in the United States of America

Contents

To my wife, April.

Preface:
Why I Wrote This Book

The radical project is not new. The last century is littered with the corpses of tens of millions of victims of the social justice warriors. Their crimes? Refusing to give up their freedoms; standing in the way of the progressive future. Like their predecessors, today's utopians imagine a future framed by group identities, and state control of economic and social activity. In other words, the precise framework of the collectivist systems that have resulted in unparalleled human catastrophes in the past, and failed.

The work of social revolutionaries inevitably begins with acts of destruction designed to undermine and eventually obliterate the foundations of the old social order. This destruction invariably starts with an act of defamation that discredits and desecrates the nation's founding and the historical heritage of the nation's past. Once deprived of the pride citizens derive from these institutional memories, a nation becomes powerless to defend itself.

In typical revolutionary fashion, the current attacks on America's heritage begin with malicious slanders intended to turn the American dream of equality and freedom into a "white supremacist" nightmare. We are told America, from its inception, has been a "racist" nation that treats minorities as less than human. In short, it deserves to be destroyed. This is now the official doctrine of the Biden White House, the "woke" Pentagon, the Democratic Senate, and the curricula of American schools.

I wrote this book to provide a concise, easily digested and accurate history of race in America to serve as an antidote to the hateful lies progressives have promoted about their own country. These lies, emanating from the President himself, describe the world's free-est, most tolerant and inclusive nation as "white supremacist" and "systemically racist." But if America were, in fact, white supremacist, the words "white" and "Black" would appear in its Constitution. They don't. If America were systemically racist, there would be a torrent of lawsuits and multi-billion-dollar judgements for damages against its racist institutions, under the Civil Rights Act of 1964, which specifically makes systemic racism a crime. But there is no such torrent, because there is no systemic racism. The accusations are lies.

To defend our country, patriotic Americans need to have a firm grip on the facts of their heritage. In particular, they need to understand that America never was a racist nation. Slavery was an African practice and the slaves exported to America were enslaved by Black Africans and sold at auctions to Europeans. The American nation, on the other hand, was born with a revolutionary declaration that liberty is a God-given right—for all. The African import of slavery was abolished in the Northern states within twenty years of the constitutional founding, and within seventy-six years in the South. This was far from the "400 years" claimed by its ignorant and malice-driven enemies. Three hundred and sixty thousand mainly white Union soldiers sacrificed their lives to free Black Africans enslaved by their brothers.

In all history, there is no other example of one race making such sacrifices to free another.

In sum: Slavery in North America was an English implant and the extension of an African business. It was not about racial oppression. Race only became an issue when Southern slaveowners, attempting to justify slavery in a nation dedicated to the proposition that all men are created equal, chose to argue that Blacks were not equal. This racist defense of the indefensible became popular in the 1830s. What was distinctly American in these arguments was the declaration of equality embraced by the American majority, not the racist defense of slavery by the soon to be defeated slave-owning minority.

Given the prejudices and bigotries that are endemic to human beings of all races, Americans can be proud of their racial past and its contribution to human freedom, and especially the freedom of African Americans. The raw facts are these: Black Africans enslaved their brothers and sisters. White Americans freed them. Slavery in North America was a system inherited from the British, which most Americans opposed from the beginning and proceeded to abolish through the greatest human sacrifices in their history, in little over a generation.

From America's inception there was always a white movement of dedicated abolitionists, many of whom were willing to give their lives to win freedom for all Blacks. There never was a successful revolt by the slaves themselves. If white Americans had been universally racist as leftists maintain, Blacks in America would still be slaves. Instead, thanks to the sacrifices of white Americans, they are the most prosperous, most privileged, and free-est Blacks in the world today, including all of Black Africa and the West Indies.

I have framed this history with a description of Martin Luther's under-appreciated role in creating the indispensable principles on which any free society must be founded, and which America's, in particular, was. I did this so that readers would understand the conditions of their freedom, and be better able to defend the principles that underlie them, which are currently under malicious attack. I have begun the text with a self-introduction, so that readers may understand the narrator of this history, and better judge the veracity of his claims.

Part One

The Priesthood of All Believers

The longer I have been in this world, which is eighty-five years and counting, the more I am impressed by an observation made almost two centuries earlier by the philosopher-theologian Søren Kierkegaard. If an aging memory serves, what Kierkegaard said was this: "The tragedy of life is that it is lived forwards but understood backwards." An equally true observation might be this: It can take eighty-five years for the isolated incidents of one man's biography to unlock the enigma of a lifetime.

Kierkegaard's religion was Lutheran—the most important of the Protestant denominations that were part of the Reformation. Until my eighteenth year, Luther and the religion he founded had existed only on the periphery of my awareness. At the time, I was a sophomore in college and had taken a summer job with the US Forest Service in St. Maries, Idaho, a mountain town in the panhandle of the state. I had signed up to work on a "blister rust control" crew whose job it was to string grid lines along the mountainsides, and then clear weeds that were hosts to the blister rust fungus, which left to itself would infect and kill the glorious pines that sheltered their slopes.

During my stay in St. Maries, I became acquainted with some locals who happened to attend a Lutheran church. In circumstances I no longer remember, I requested and received an invitation to preach a Sunday sermon to their congregation. This put me in touch with Americans who were still following the inspirational teachings of the Christian monk, five centuries after his death.

My appearance in the Lutheran pulpit might seem a particularly odd one for a Jew, and a Marxist. But the family I grew up in was somewhat deracinated, as it is the universal disposition of radicals to be. After all, if you are seeking to "change the world" and ready to dismantle all its structures in the service of your transformative designs, why wouldn't rootlessness be a second nature?

The secularists who raised me had a spiritual home in the Soviet Union, which was already a bloody prison whose realities they refused to acknowledge, and whose atrocities they were certain had not taken place. As was I, their dutiful and loyal son. Young as I was, I had already pledged my energy and talents to furthering their progressive crusade to save the world. As far as my parents and their friends were concerned, religious belief was superstition, a relic of the ignorant and oppressive past, which an enlightened mankind would soon discard.

Though I never broached the subject with them, I was sure they looked on my Christian flirtations as something my youthful self would outgrow. It was a facet of their loyalty to their son. To the ends of their lives, on the other hand, it never occurred to them that their revolutionary passion to save the world was also a religious belief, and that its followers were as encumbered by superstition and ignorance as some followers of the creeds they so haughtily despised.

I was born in 1939, and the Nazi Holocaust of the Jews framed the circumstances of my youth. My parents probably looked at my affinity for Christian ideas as an insurance that I might be protected from the hostile inclinations of our Christian neighbors. In any case, because my parents had detached themselves from their Jewish roots, and I was firmly committed to the alien faith they had adopted, they did not raise an eyebrow when I told them I considered myself a "Christian romantic." (In my mind, calling myself a "romantic" insulated me from the charge that I had become an actual believer.) The phrase was a metaphor, whose heroic overtones served to flatter my youthful ambitions.

I was indeed taken with the story of Jesus as the son of God, who was sacrificed by his Father so that a sinful mankind could live. Equally attractive was the fact that Jesus was crucified by the Roman authorities because his followers looked on him as the "King of the Jews." They saw his failure to worship their idols as a subversive challenge to their imperial rule. Jesus's fate was that of an iconic rebel against the tyranny of an all-powerful state—an irresistible model for an aspiring revolutionary like me.

The neighborhood I grew up in was working class, its families mainly Italian and Irish Catholics. My fearful mother instructed me to be respectful to our Christian neighbors, who were dedicated anti-Communists and not especially fond of Jews. The Catholics my parents hated most were Senator Joseph McCarthy and Bishop Fulton J. Sheen, a TV figure whose intelligence and lucid lectures were a source of guilty fascination for me. Whether my mother's fears were aroused by the anti-Communist passions of our Catholic neighbors, or their occasional anti-Semitic actions, I never really knew.

Thanks to my mother's concerns, I grew up in an oddly insular environment. She felt that secrets were the way to protect the innocent. But they also had unintended effects. If you don't know who is making a silent case against you while pretending to be your friend, how can you protect yourself when their hatred bursts into the open? When the neighborhood kids I thought were friends stole my baseball equipment or left me behind when our neighborhood ball team went to see the Yankees play, I was totally unaware of their calculated malice, and didn't find out until my mother decided to reveal the dark secret to me as an adult. When she finally told me, the truth still hurt, but it hurt less and it was too late to do anything about it.

When I arrived in St. Maries, I was mindful to follow my mother's counsel and show respect to the Christian locals. This helps to explain how I approached the members of a Lutheran congregation, who then invited me to deliver a Sunday sermon in their church.

My sermon was built around a story that captured the Christian message and also resonated with my family's mission as self-appointed saviors of mankind. For its text I chose "The Happy Prince," a poignant tale by the nineteenth-century author Oscar Wilde. Wilde was a witty and persecuted homosexual, who suffered greatly from the bigoted attitudes of his fellow Christians, including imprisonment and humiliation for his sexual desires. Even today, I cannot retell the story of the Happy Prince without a welling of tears, as I am touched by sadness for our common human fate, which condemns us to search in vain for solace and redemption in this mortal life.

The Happy Prince

The Happy Prince was a majestic statue rising above the town square of an unnamed European city. His eyes were sapphires and his body was gilded over with leaves of fine gold. He wore a sword with a red ruby that glowed on its hilt.

As winter approached, a little swallow dallied by a river, while his friends took off to spend the winter in the warm environs of Egypt. Eventually, the swallow accepted the fact that winter was coming and that he must set out to join his friends among the pyramids, and bathe in the warmth of the desert sun.

By chance, the swallow's first stop was the place where the Happy Prince stood tall over the city square. The day was ending and the swallow was tired, and when he saw the statue he alighted at the Prince's feet, and prepared to sleep. But just as he was putting his head under his wing, a drop of water fell on him. It was the Prince, and he was crying. "Who are you?" said the swallow.

"I am the Happy Prince," the statue replied. "Then why are you weeping?" the swallow asked.

"When I was alive and had a human heart," the Prince answered, "I did not know what tears were, for I lived in the Palace of Without Cares, where sorrow is not allowed to enter. Now that I am dead, they have set me up here so high that I can see all the ugliness and all the misery of my city, and though my heart is made of lead yet I cannot choose but weep." Then the Happy Prince asked the swallow if he would be his messenger and help a poor seamstress whose son was lying ill with a fever. The little boy was asking for oranges, but his mother had nothing to give him but river water, so he was crying. "Swallow, swallow, little Swallow," said the Happy Prince, "will you not bring her the ruby out of my sword hilt? My feet are fastened to this pedestal and I cannot move."

"I am waited for in Egypt," said the swallow.

"Swallow, swallow, little swallow," said the Prince, "will you not stay with me for one night, and be my messenger? The boy is so thirsty, and the mother so sad."

The little swallow was moved by the Prince's request. "It is very cold here," he said; "but I will stay with you for one night, and be your messenger."

When the swallow came to the seamstress's house, the boy was tossing feverishly on his bed, and the mother had fallen asleep. He laid the great ruby on the table beside the woman's thimble. Then he flew gently round the bed, fanning the boy's forehead with his wings. "How cool I feel," said the boy, "I must be getting better;" and he sank into a delicious slumber.

Then the swallow flew back to the Happy Prince, and told him what he had done. "It is curious," he remarked, "but I feel quite warm now, although it is so cold."

"That is because you have done something good," said the Prince. The next day the swallow said to the Prince, "Tonight I go to Egypt."

"Swallow, swallow, little swallow," said the Prince, "will you not stay with me one night longer? Far across the city, there is a young man in a garret who is writing a play but is too cold to finish it. There is no fire in the grate, and hunger has made him faint."

"I will wait with you one night longer," said the swallow, who really had a good heart. "Shall I take him another ruby?"

"Alas! I have no ruby now," said the Prince; "my eyes are all that I have left. They are made of rare sapphires, which were brought out of India a thousand years ago. Pluck out one of them and take it to him. He will sell it to the jeweler, and buy food and firewood, and finish his play."

"Dear Prince," said the swallow, "I cannot do that"; and he began to weep.

"Swallow, swallow, little swallow," said the Prince, "do as I command you."

So the swallow plucked out the Prince's eye, and flew away to the student's garret. When the young man found the beautiful sapphire, he cried "I am beginning to be appreciated. This is from some great admirer. Now I can finish my play."

The next day the swallow flew back to the Prince. "I am come to bid you good-bye," he said.

"Swallow, swallow, little swallow," said the Prince, "will you not stay with me one night longer?"

"It is winter," answered the Swallow, "and the chill snow will soon be here. In Egypt the sun is warm on the green palm-trees, and the crocodiles lie in the mud and look lazily about them. My companions are building a nest in the Temple of Baalbec, and the pink and white doves are watching them, and cooing to each other. Dear Prince, I must leave you, but I will never forget you, and next spring I will bring you back two beautiful jewels in place of those you have given away. The ruby shall be redder than a red rose, and the sapphire shall be as blue as the great sea."

"In the square below," said the Prince, "there stands a little match-girl. She has let her matches fall in the gutter, and they are all spoiled. Her father will beat her if she does not bring home some money, and she is crying. She has no shoes or stockings, and her little head is bare. Pluck out my other eye, and give it to her, and her father will not beat her."

"I will stay with you one night longer," said the swallow, "but I cannot pluck out your eye. You would be quite blind then."

"Swallow, swallow, little swallow," said the Prince, "do as I command you."

So he plucked out the Prince's other eye, and darted down with it. He swooped past the match-girl, and slipped the jewel into the palm of her hand. "What a lovely bit of glass," cried the little girl; and she ran home, laughing.

Then the swallow came back to the Prince. "You are blind now," he said, "so I will stay with you always."

"No, little swallow," said the poor Prince, "you must go away to Egypt."

"I will stay with you always," said the swallow, and he slept at the Prince's feet.

All the next day he sat on the Prince's shoulder, and told him stories of what he had seen in strange lands.

"Dear little swallow," said the Prince, "you tell me of marvelous things, but more marvelous than anything is the suffering of men and of women. There is no Mystery so great as Misery. Fly over my city, little swallow, and tell me what you see there."

So the swallow flew over the great city, and saw the rich making merry in their beautiful houses, while the beggars were sitting at the gates. He flew into dark lanes, and saw the white faces of starving children looking out listlessly at the Black streets. Then he flew back and told the Prince what he had seen.

"I am covered with fine gold," said the Prince, "you must take it off, leaf by leaf, and give it to my poor."

Leaf after leaf of the fine gold the swallow picked off, till the Prince looked quite dull and grey. Leaf after leaf of the fine gold he brought to the poor, and the children's faces grew rosier, and they laughed and played games in the street. "We have bread now!" they cried.

Then the snow came, and after the snow came the frost. The poor little swallow grew colder and colder, but he would not leave the Prince; he loved him too well. He picked up crumbs outside the baker's door and tried to keep himself warm by flapping his wings. But at last, he knew that he was going to die. He had just strength to fly up to the Prince's shoulder once more. "Good-bye, dear Prince!" he murmured, "will you let me kiss your hand?"

"I am glad that you are going to Egypt at last, little swallow," said the Prince, "you have stayed too long here; but you must kiss me on the lips, for I love you."

"It is not to Egypt that I am going," said the swallow. "I am going to the House of Death. Death is the brother of Sleep, is he not?"

And he kissed the Happy Prince on the lips, and fell down dead at his feet.

At that moment a curious crack sounded inside the statue, as if something had broken.

The fact is that the leaden heart had snapped right in two.

Wilde ends his story with God taking the Prince's broken heart along with his dead swallow friend to be with Him in heaven.

The Longing for Redemption

To me this little fable was a faithful rendition of the Christian faith, expressed in this passage of the gospel of John: "God so loved the world, he gave his only begotten Son, that whosoever believeth on him should not perish, but have eternal life."[1]

What attracted me to the Wilde tale, and still stirs my emotions, is the way it accurately reflects this most powerful impulse within us: to love and help others; to treat strangers as part of one human family, and to transform the world from its seemingly insuperable conflicts and sufferings into a harmonious, friendly, and liberating place. I did not feel this desire was special to Christians and denied to Jews. After all, the creators of Christianity—Jesus and Paul—were Jews. I felt this compassionate outlook applied also to my atheist parents who were Communists, who judged individuals harshly but who wanted to save them all, and who had somehow transmitted their missionary fervor to me.

---

1   http://www.growingdisciples.org/Sermons/Generous%20Love.htm

I concluded my sermon with a famous passage from Paul's letter to the Corinthians. Again, I did not feel I was betraying my fellow Jews in quoting Paul, because when he wrote these words, Christianity was still a Jewish faith— albeit a rebel one. Moreover, the days when Christians burned Jews at the stake to force their conversion were long buried in the Medieval past.

Here is what the apostle Paul wrote: "Though I speak with the tongues of men and of angels, and have not charity, I am become as sounding brass, or a tinkling cymbal. And though I have the gift of prophecy, and understand all mysteries, and all knowledge; and though I have all faith, so that I could remove mountains, and have not charity, I am nothing. . . ."[2]

Luther and Me

Martin Luther was still just a Christian name to me. I knew he was instrumental in the Protestant Reformation and had challenged the corruption of the Roman Church. But he remained a hazy figure in my mind until some years later, when I became aware of his hatred for the Jews. This hatred was intense and produced a well of hostility in me. I despised him for it and returned his hate.

---

2   https://biblehub.com/kjv/1_corinthians/13.htm

The hostility lasted for several decades until my understanding of the man changed just as dramatically. One lever of this change was my discovery of how Luther's initial feelings towards the Jews were actually quite compassionate. In the beginning, his attitude was kind and empathetic. He approached Jews with a self-critical regret at the way Christians treated them. When all was said and done, Judaism was a kindred faith.

In 1519, Luther wrote: "Absurd theologians defend hatred for the Jews. What Jew would consent to enter our ranks when he sees the cruelty and enmity we wreak on them—that in our behavior towards them we less resemble Christians than beasts?"[3] Four years later he wrote an essay titled "That Jesus Christ Was Born a Jew,"[4] in which he condemned the inhumane treatment of the Jews and urged Christians to treat them with Christian charity. I admired the honesty and courage of this—the way Luther was able to see Jews as the human beings they were and not be consumed by the abstractions of hate.

But Luther also had an ulterior motive; he hoped that he might convert the Jews to his Christian belief that Jesus was the messiah, the savior of mankind. When the Jews stubbornly resisted his overtures and refused to give up their faith, he turned on them with a vengeance. Now

---

3   https://www.ariel.org/assets/documents/outlines/o-hht.pdf?updated
    =1613014659

4   https://ccjr.us/dialogika-resources/primary-texts-from-the-history-of-the
    -relationship/luther-1523

his attitude was so ferociously antagonistic, and his writing about them so filled with venom that he became the foremost German precursor of the Nazis and exerted a powerful influence over the forces of Jew hatred among his countrymen, which led to the Final Solution, and the Jews' darkest hour.

Twenty years later, when he was at the height of his influence, Luther wrote a book he titled *On the Jews and Their Lies*, in which he deplored Christendom's failure to expel them.[5] "What shall we Christians do with this rejected and condemned people, the Jews?" he asked. And then answered with what can only be described as a tribal anathema:

> "First, to set fire to their synagogues or schools . . . This is to be done in honor of our Lord and of Christendom, so that God might see that we are Christians . . ."
>
> "Second, I advise that their houses also be razed and destroyed."
>
> "Third, I advise that all their prayer books and Talmudic writings, in which such idolatry, lies, cursing, and blasphemy are taught, be taken from them."
>
> "Fourth, I advise that their rabbis be forbidden to teach henceforth on pain of loss of life and limb . . ."[6]

---

5   https://www.prchiz.pl/storage/app/media/pliki/Luther_On_Jews.pdf

6   https://www.jewishvirtuallibrary.org/martin-luther-quot-the-jews-and-their
     -lies-quot

I hated Luther for this screed. I hated him for his hatred. I hated him on behalf of my fellow Jews who perished in the Holocaust, and I hated him for the seeds he planted of Holocausts to come.

If you had told me then or for half a century afterwards that I would come to see another side of this famous monk and his achievements; if you told me I would come to understand him in a way that would put me forever in awe of what he had accomplished, and cause me to appreciate how he had made life for everyone who lived under the canopy of his ideas better—including and especially my persecuted tribe—how he made them freer, safer, and more at home in the world; if you had told me in my twenties that sixty years later I would come to see him as one of freedom's greatest heroes, I would have laughed and said: you are mad.

Martin Luther's genocidal hatred of the Jews is a lesson that believers are not immune from human sin—from redirecting their mission to the service of evil. "Men never do evil so completely and cheerfully," observed the great Catholic thinker, Blaise Pascal, "as when they do it from religious conviction."[7] As when they put a God imagined by human beings—a political party, a charismatic leader, a "sacred" ideal—before the image of a true divinity, one they cannot manipulate or control.

---

7 http://justus.anglican.org/resources/bio/233.html

Two Types of Faith

Secular messianism—progressive hope—is a religious conviction. That is why good, intelligent, and otherwise caring people have colluded in creating the cruelest regimes that ever existed. The Communist Gulag was the work of evil men. But it could not have been created, or survive as long as it did, without the active collusion of good men and women, secular and religious, who were seduced by its beautiful vision of a just world. This paradox is a warning that the aspiration of human beings to remake the world from the bottom up is a dangerous and destructive fantasy.

The Communist faith in which my parents raised me was a secular version of the Judeo-Christian idea. We did not believe in a God who was the Creator. But in everything else our faith resembled that of the believers. Like them, we saw the world as blighted by corruption, and we searched the horizon for a Promised Land that would be harmonious and just. The difference was that our Promised Land was located in this life, not in the next.

As Communists, we, too, believed that evil and oppression were everywhere. But while Christians and Jews believed that evil was embedded in the human soul and that life was a constant struggle to subdue and control it, we social redeemers believed that the corruption was rooted in an external reality called "society." The father of the modern Left, Jean-Jacques Rousseau, famously summed up this idea in the following words: "Man is born free, but is everywhere in chains."[8]

Like our religious counterparts, we looked to a coming redemption—one that we alone could make possible; a redemption that would end human suffering and create harmony between its warring individuals and tribes. Religious Christians and Jews believed this result was impossible because the source of our misery lay within us. Therefore, the redemption could only be the work of a merciful divinity. Human beings could not liberate themselves from evil because human beings were the source of the evil.

The community I grew up in was composed of social revolutionaries who didn't believe in human sin or a redeeming God. We believed the redemption of the world would be our work. Our arrogance—and with it our capacity for making things infinitely worse—was that great. We would act as gods and re-create the world. Against all logic, we believed that the source of our miseries, which was human nature, could be the solution.

Consider how absurd is this view: By empowering a revolutionary "vanguard" to act as gods and recreate the world, we believed we could achieve a humane and just future. How could we have ever believed this? How could we believe that the same human beings whose greed, deceit, envy, bigotry, sadism, and hate were responsible for human misery could liberate the world if only they

---

8 https://mn.gov/mnddc/parallels/three/2.html#

could acquire enough power to compel everyone else to obey them? Was there ever a more perverse and destructive idea? There never was.

To this obvious misery we added a new dimension of perversity. To seek the redemption of the world was a holy mission. Indeed, what mission could be nobler? Therefore, what lie would our social justice warriors not tell, what crime not commit or support, to achieve such a miraculous result? Our radical utopianism was a criminal creed.

Once one shook off the self-delusions of the righteous, what remained was so obviously sinister. How do human beings seeking an earthly redemption destroy the beautiful world of their dreams? They pursue those dreams ferociously, as if nothing else mattered. They pursue them by putting themselves first, and silencing their critics. They pursue a world that they perceive to be just, when others do not. They rationalize their crimes by believing that the end justifies the means. They pursue their noble ideals by coveting, lying, cheating, stealing, and killing. And no commandments can stop them.

The wisdom that refutes this self-deception is as old as mankind. *Thou shalt have no other Gods before me.* No other Gods: Not the party, not the Church, not the State, not the revolution, not its leaders, not its sacred rules, beliefs, idols. Not anything.

But of course, in the redeemers' eyes, every "servant" of the revolution is his or her own god, setting out to recreate the world, and make it "a better place."

To a man and woman, those of us who broke free from these utopian delusions came to understand that the corrupter of the world was not society; patriarchy; or race. It was us.

These truths are encapsulated in the most humbling and liberating Lutheran doctrine of all: Justification by Faith.[9] This phrase encapsulates the belief that one cannot earn a place in heaven by good works because there is not a soul among us who deserves to be saved. We are selfish and self-centered; greedy and deceitful, malicious and cruel. Therefore, if we are to be saved at all, it can only be by divine grace.

This was the idea that Martin Luther put front and center in his thoughts about the human condition. The idea itself was not original with him. It was central to being a Christian. Yet it was denied by the Roman Church's offer of indulgences as a means to salvation. This was the devil in the detail that set Luther on his revolutionary course. An institution, like the Church, created and managed by mere mortals, could have no authority to decide who should or should not be saved. Salvation could be achieved by faith and God's grace alone.

To Christians, belief in a savior who died on the cross to pay for mankind's sins was the only possible path to redemption: "For it is by grace you have been saved

---

9 https://www.christianstudylibrary.org/article/martin-luther-and-doctrine-justification-faith-alone

through faith. It is not from yourself or anything you've done, but the gift of God." Ephesians 2:8–9

Why are human beings denied power over their own salvation? Because of who they are: selfish, untrustworthy, envious, jealous, covetous, devious, ignorant, and cruel. Even an agnostic can appreciate this truth. If redemption is possible, if a harmonious world can be achieved, it will not be by the efforts of those who are the source of human misery but only by the grace of a God whom mortals cannot seduce or corrupt.

As it happens, this is also the foundational belief of a secular democracy, based on equality and individual freedom. No institution such as the state—created and run by human beings—can be trusted to guarantee basic human rights. Therefore, none must have the authority to take them away. These rights must be seen as a gift from God, and therefore unalienable.

Luther and the Church

The writer Aleksander Solzhenitsyn was the greatest individual adversary of Communism and its totalitarian empire. "One man who stopped lying, could bring down a tyranny," he famously said.[10] And in a way he did bring down that tyranny. In writing the *Gulag Archipalego,*

---

10 https://academyofideas.com/2021/09/the-big-lie-how-to-enslave-the-world/

Solzhenitsyn risked his life to expose the hateful truth of the Communist future, and the walls came tumbling down.

Though Martin Luther lived half a millennium before the Russian, his achievement was no different and in fact much greater. He was the instigator of the Protestant Reformation which destroyed the absolute authority of the Holy Roman Empire and created in these liberating ideas—the sanctity of the individual and equality—the foundations of the free world.

Just as Solzhenitsyn was a dedicated Communist before the scales fell from his eyes, so Martin Luther was a devout Catholic before he brought the Church to its knees. In its own perception, the Church was an institution of divine origin—founded by Jesus, and deriving its authority from Him. To establish this *bona fide*, the Church authorities drew on a scripture from the Gospel of Matthew. In it, Jesus addresses his disciple Peter, and makes him the first Pope. "I tell you, you are Peter, and on this rock I will build my Church, and the gates of hell shall not prevail against it. I will give you the keys of the kingdom of heaven, and whatever you bind on earth shall be bound in heaven, and whatever you loose on earth shall be loosed in heaven."[11]

In the Church's theology, the Catholic popes were said to receive the keys to heaven directly from Peter, and then his successors. Thus, by a divine imprimatur, the Papal Authority, a temporal institution, was elevated above its

11 https://www.bible.com/bible/compare/MAT.16.18-19

mortal rivals. To oppose the Papal Authority, as Martin Luther was about to do, was heresy. The punishment for the transgression: death by burning.

Luther was a devoted servant of the Church. But as he reached his thirty-fourth year, he could no longer avert his eyes from the fact that the Church he loved was deeply immersed in human corruption. This corruption was so grievous that it put the Holy See in dramatic conflict with its own teachings and those of the very Scriptures from which its authority derived.

The sins of the Church were crystalized in the sale of "indulgences"—passes to heaven for sinners serving punitive time in purgatory.[12] In other words, a shortcut to salvation. The offer itself was a stepping-in for God, a decision as to who should be saved and who should be left to suffer for their mortal misdeeds.

This practice arrogated to the ordinary mortals of the priesthood the power of divine grace. It was, in practice, a theft of the divine in the service of human vice, which is the foundation of most human tyrannies. It elevated the priesthood and the Church to superhuman heights, and set them over the ordinary souls who formed their congregations, and now depended on their indulgences.

Luther's revolt began with a loyal appeal to the Pope to end the unholy practice. But the Papal Authority was so dependent on the profits from selling salvation that it refused his request, and continued to suborn divine grace

---

12 https://www.britannica.com/topic/indulgence

for its own profit. The Church's refusal brought Luther into irreconcilable conflict with the institution he loved. The collision changed the world.

The Church's Corruption

There should have been no surprise in this conflict and its results. A thousand years earlier, the Church, then a small, beleaguered flock of the followers of Jesus, agreed to become the official religion of the Roman Empire—henceforth the Holy Roman Empire. What could one expect from such a marriage? Its clerical and worldly heads now controlled the fate of all individuals within their purview, both in this life and in the next. With this marriage of Church and State, the once tiny following of Christians came to encompass the known world, and the malign influences of that world infected and corrupted their moral purpose.

In Luther's time, the Catholic Pope was Leo X, who was born Giovanni de Lorenzo de Medici, and was the scion of the wealthiest family in Europe. When he was only thirteen years old, Lorenzo was made a Cardinal of the Church. He became Pope in 1513, continuing his lavish lifestyle from the seat of the papacy. Within two years of becoming Pope, he had drained the treasury amassed by his frugal predecessor. When he died in 1521, he left the papal treasury 400,000 ducats in debt.[13]

---

13 https://www.catholic.com/encyclopedia/pope-leo-x

As a temporal power in its own right, the Roman Church was a builder of cathedrals, the focus of its worship and power. One of its most expensive capital projects was the building of St. Peter's in Rome. The Church was also a collector of art and other treasures. In amassing them, the Medici Pope kept up his expensive family tradition. The Church was also a funder of charities and wars. Some of the "charities" were the Pope's political friends.

If you were Albrecht, the Archbishop of Magdeburg, also the papal overseer of Indulgences and the Elector of Mainz, for example, you could divert some of the revenues to become the Archbishop of Mainz and increase your personal power and wealth, which Albrecht did.

To finance all these expensive, often venal activities, the Church had come up with the ingenious scheme of Indulgences, which an unkind critic might describe as selling real estate in heaven. An Indulgence, as promoted by the Church, was a way to reduce the amount of punishment one had to undergo for sins committed. For Christians in the Middle Ages, the site of these torments was Purgatory, and the duration of their torments could be ten thousand years or more. Help was available from the only true Church, directly founded by Jesus. For a price, a sinner could buy an Indulgence and reduce the sentence dramatically, or even completely. The more one paid in advance of one's death, the shorter one's sentence would become.

Luther was beside himself over this unholy scam. The Church had arrogated to itself the power of God to grant absolution for sin, and to determine the eternal fate of His children. The goals of this practice were earthly self-aggrandizement and human corruption. By merging temporal and spiritual authorities, the Church had created a tyranny backed by God. Where was the scriptural basis for this? There was none. Indeed, where was the scriptural authority to say that the popes who followed Peter were also handed the "keys to heaven"? There was none. But the masses who funded the Church had no access to the Scriptures, which were written in Latin and thus closed to them.

Luther's Defiance

In 1517, in the famous act of defiance that launched the Protestant Reformation, Luther nailed his "95 Theses" on indulgences to the door of the Castle Church in Wittenberg.[14] Among them was this devastating question:

> 82. Why does not the Pope, whose wealth is today greater than the wealth of the richest Croesus, build this one basilica of St. Peter with his own money rather than with the money of poor believers?[15]

In exposing the empty claims of the Church to be God's authority on earth, Luther challenged the entire

---

14 https://www.luther.de/en/95thesen.html
15 https://www.luther.de/en/95thesen.html

hierarchy responsible for exploiting Catholic believers. In his Address to the Nobility of the German Nation, which was published in 1520, Luther proclaimed this revolutionary idea: "We are all consecrated as priests through baptism, as St. Peter says in Peter 2: 'You are a royal priesthood, and a priestly kingdom.'"[16]

Thus did the "priesthood of all believers" become the central liberating doctrine of the Protestant Reformation. It established a spiritual equality between believers by declaring that their relationship to God would no longer be mediated by a priesthood or a Pope or the Holy Roman Empire; no longer by mere mortals elevated above them with the power to determine their eternal fate. By declaring all believers equal, Luther had transferred spiritual power to the people themselves.

This was heresy, and on January 3, 1521, Luther was excommunicated by the Catholic Church. Five months later, the German monk was summoned to the Diet of Worms where the Holy Roman Emperor Charles V presided. At the Diet, Luther was called to recant his beliefs or be burned at the stake. He refused. This was his answer:

My conscience is captive to the Word of God. Thus, I cannot and will not recant, for going against conscience

16 https://books.google.com/books?id=OCRtDwAAQBAJ&pg=PA50 &lpg=#v=onepage&q&f=false

is neither safe nor salutary. I can do no other, here I stand, God help me. Amen.[17]

My conscience is captive to the word of God. It was a declaration of individual freedom that would resound through the annals of every struggle for freedom in the centuries to come. Every individual's freedom of conscience was an assertion of independence from temporal power. An unalienable right to think and speak freely, which derived from the individual's inviolable relation to their Creator—beyond the reach of Church or State, or any institution created by mortal human beings. No man or woman was bound to surrender their freedom of conscience to others seeking to coerce them into the service of a rival belief. Luther may not have intended the full freedom to which this proclamation led, but he had loosed the idea upon the world, and the world responded by making it the cornerstone of Protestant belief.

The Holy Roman Emperor was not pleased. Understanding Luther's claim as a direct and mortal threat to his tyrannical authority, he issued a declaration known as "The Edict of Worms," which condemned Luther to earthly damnation: "We forbid anyone from this time forward to dare, either by words or by deeds, to receive, defend, sustain, or favor the said Martin Luther. On the contrary, we want him to be apprehended and punished as a notorious heretic, as he deserves, to be brought

17 https://www.libertymagazine.org/article/the-scripturally-informed-conscience

personally before us, or to be securely guarded until those who have captured him inform us, whereupon we will order the appropriate manner of proceeding against the said Luther. Those who will help in his capture will be rewarded generously for their good work."[18]

Further edicts also condemned Luther and officially banned citizens of the Holy Roman Empire from defending or spreading his ideas. The penalty for doing so was to forfeit all property, half of which would be confiscated by the imperial government while the remaining half would be given as a reward to the party who brought the accusation.

Luther was now a hunted man. If caught, his fate was to be burned at the stake. Luther's supporters helped him flee to the castle of a friend, where he spent the next year translating the New Testament into German.

The Reformation Is a Democratization

This was a revolutionary act in itself at a time when the Scriptures were available only in Latin, Aramaic, and Greek. Translating the New Testament into the vernacular put the Word of God directly into the hands of the people. For the first time, they could judge for themselves what their Savior intended, and could distinguish

---

18 https://www.crivoice.org/creededictworms.html

His Gospel from what merely served the self-interests of power-hungry, deceitful men.

By a stroke of good fortune, the publication of Luther's New Testament in thousands of copies was made possible by a recent, epoch-making, technological revolution: the invention of the printing press. Along with a New Testament accessible to everyone, this also made possible the widespread distribution of Luther's 95 Theses, and the pamphlets in which he explained his vision that all believers were equal in the eyes of their Creator, communicated directly with Him, and in matters of conscience were beholden only to Him.

This egalitarian view, widely distributed through the new printing technology, made Luther a popular hero to masses of people. This provided him with a wide base of support that protected him from the powers of Church and State in a way that previous heretics like the martyred Jan Hus were not. His views championed the right of believers to have direct access to the Scriptures which were—or should have been—the foundation of their faith. The printing of the Gospels and Luther's tracts—all in accessible German—enabled multitudes to draw conclusions for themselves on the most important issues of their religion.

In the years that followed, as the Reformation spread through northern Europe and beyond, literacy and education powered its growth. The Protestant dedication to both was so intense that even hundreds of years after Luther's death, the literacy rates in Protestant countries exceed those in Catholic countries by as much as

20 percent.[19] Their encouragement of public education generally, and the education of women in particular, created a true leveling revolution between masses and elites, and an unprecedented empowerment of individuals, providing them with the tools for weighing their options, and the freedom to determine their fates.

19 https://novellearning.blog/2022/09/05/protestantism-raised-literacy /; https://onlinelibrary.wiley.com/doi/10.1111/socf.12250

Part Two

A Democratic Nation

Three centuries after Luther's death, a schism among English Protestants led to the creation of the first modern democratic nation in North America. This rift between the British crown and its English colonies began as a complaint about mundane issues like a tax on tea, but escalated into the sweeping embrace of a much grander vision: the sanctity of individual conscience, and the equality of all.

In the crucible of Luther's ideas and actions a new nation was born. Having stripped the one true Church—and therefore any "true" church—of divine authority, his ideas had given birth to a nation conceived in liberty and dedicated to human equality and freedom.

From the moment Luther nailed his "95 Theses" to the door of the Wittenberg Cathedral, he struck a chord in the hearts of ordinary men and women. His ideas were so powerful that that they led directly to America's Declaration of Independence, in which colonies composed of 98 percent Protestant Christians announced the creation of a revolutionary democracy based on individual freedoms that were bestowed by their Creator.[20] There was henceforth no True Church, and therefore no government in America that was ordained and authorized by God to rule over others. There was only government authorized to regulate human behaviors by ordinary individuals whose souls would always belong to their Creator.

In ending the reign of the One True Church, Luther had given rise to a myriad of religious denominations. According to the World Christian Encyclopedia, as of 2001, the number of Protestant denominations worldwide exceeded thirty-three thousand, with about 270 new ones every year or five every week.[21] But in 1776, in America, the number was still relatively small—mainly Lutherans, Puritans, Quakers, Congregationalists, German Reformed, and Deists, but also others seeking refuge in a new world wilderness. It was a cacophony of sects, which is what individual freedom looks like.

In his treatise *Secular Authority: To What Extent It Should Be Obeyed*, Luther explained the thinking behind

---

20 https://www.archives.gov/founding-docs/declaration-transcript

21 https://www.christianitytoday.com/ct/topics/d/denominations/; https
    ://urbanministries.com/globally-there-are-33000-different-christian
    -denominations/; https://www.catholic.com/qa/how-can-we-respond-to
    -the-call-no-man-father-question; https://books.google.com/books?id
    =t0IWBAAAQBAJ&pg=PA17&lpg#v=onepage&q&f=false

his doctrines of limited ecclesiastical and state authority. This came to be known as his "two kingdoms" theology, which outlined the theological foundations of the separation of Church and State:

> Worldly government has laws which extend no farther than to life and property and what is external upon earth. For over the soul God can and will let no one rule but Himself. Therefore, where earthly power presumes to prescribe laws for the soul, it encroaches upon God's government and only misleads and destroys the souls.[22]

The sanctity of the human soul: This is the foundation of all democracy and the nemesis of human tyranny. *My conscience is captive to the word of God.*

In 1776, the English-speaking Protestants in North America were a gathering of thirteen distinctive colonies. Lutheran values were so central to the Reformation and the beliefs of these settlers that the colonial rivals to England's empire building—the Spanish imperialists who were Catholics, and who had already conquered Florida—referred to all Protestants as "Lutherans."

They had established their communities in a spacious territory that provided breathing room for free men and women, and a foundation on which their flocks were bound to expand. Some of the colonies were repressive

---

22 https://www.patheos.com/blogs/geneveith/2015/01/luther-madison-and-the
  -two-kingdoms/; https://www.libertymagazine.org/article/the-scripturally
  -informed-conscience#

theocracies—replicas of the societies that had cast them out. Others were liberal and tolerant and even inclusive enough to embrace the native "Indians" in their religious services. They were models of the directions in which Protestantism was destined to evolve.

As the conflicts with Anglican England came to a head, the colonists were eventually impressed with the fact that they had to form a union for self-defense. This meant the colonies that still held onto the idea of a theocratic state and an established Church had to abandon such aspirations. It also meant that they had to create a secular state to preside over a society composed of diverse religious believers. This would forestall any attempt to raise one denomination over the others. It meant respecting the limits Luther had drawn for the Two Kingdoms—religious and political—resulting in limited powers for both authorities. This was a radical step of such import that it remains a resonant force that inspires people seeking freedom all over the world, two and half centuries later.

Luther's insight impressed James Madison, the principal author of the First Amendment to the Bill of Rights. This cornerstone of American democracy sets a boundary beyond which the power of the state may not pass and guarantees freedom of conscience and its expression.[23]

---

23 Martin Luther, "An Appeal to the Ruling Class," 383; Miller, Nicholas P. *The Religious Roots of the First Amendment* (p. 186). Oxford University Press, Kindle Edition.

In 1821, Madison wrote a letter to the pastor of the Lutheran Missouri Synod expressing admiration for his liberality in a recent sermon, and his own gratitude for Martin Luther's insight into creating a polity reflective of such values: "It is a pleasing and persuasive example of pious zeal, united with pure benevolence, and of a cordial attachment to a particular creed untinctured with sectarian illiberality."[24] In other words, Luther's values were an example of how people with passionate but divergent beliefs could coexist with others. Or, as Madison framed the thought:

> It illustrates the excellence of a system which, by a due distinction to which the genius and courage of Luther led the way, between what is due to Caesar and what is due to God, best promotes the discharge of both obligations.[25]

Madison then described his own achievement, based on the same principles:

> The experience of the United States is a happy disproof of the error so long rooted in the unenlightened mind of well-meaning Christians as well as in the corrupt hearts of persecuting usurpers, that without a legal

---

24 https://www.patheos.com/blogs/geneveith/2015/01/luther-madison-and-the -two-kingdoms/; https://founders.archives.gov/documents/Madison/04-02 -02-0357

25 https://www.patheos.com/blogs/geneveith/2015/01/luther-madison-and-the -two-kingdoms/; https://www.beliefnet.com/faiths/faith-tools/the-founding -faith-archive/james-madison/letter-from-james-madison-to-fl-schaeffer-1.aspx

incorporation of religious and civil polity, neither could be supported.[26]

The separation of Church and State; the idea of equality embodied in the doctrine of "the priesthood of all believers";[27] the respect for, and protection of, the principle of human diversity and therefore, the idea of mutual respect for difference; and the sanctity and freedom of individual conscience—these are all ideas that can be traced to Martin Luther's revolt against the oppression and corruption of the Catholic Church and its role as a sanctifier of the Holy Roman Empire.

Because his ideas resonated with large masses of people, their influence sometimes led to conflicting and contradictory results. Luther himself did not fully embrace the powerful guarantees of human freedom embodied in the US Constitution, as witnessed by his attitude toward the Jews. But the better angels of his nature inspired the attitudes that created the constitutional order of the first liberal society in human history.

Luther's principles provided the keys to a world-transforming revolution, reining in the powers of Church and State—the two institutions historically responsible for the tyranny of the few over the many, thus

---

26 https://www.patheos.com/blogs/geneveith/2015/01/luther-madison-and-the -two-kingdoms/; https://www.revolutionary-war-and-beyond.com/james -madison-quotes-8.html

27 https://history.hanover.edu/hhr/18/HHR2018-estes.pdf; https://credomag .com/2020/01/luthers-doctrine-of-the-priesthood-of-all-believers-the -importance-for-today/

creating a critical space for the creation of a society of free individuals.

Capping these revolutionary principles was the heart of Martin Luther's stand before the Holy Roman Emperor at the Diet of Worms, the principle on which he wagered his life: "My conscience is captive to the Word of God" [28]—therefore inviolable and sacrosanct.

What can this mean for the inhabitants of a secular society, many of whom are not believers? Is a personal relationship with a divinity necessary for recognizing the sanctity of an individual life? Why should it be? Even those of us who are agnostics or atheists resort to religious language to express our feelings about spectacular and otherwise inexplicable aspects of our reality as well as to characterize their importance to us. We refer to the "miracle of birth," when a child is born—especially if it is our own child. This phrase captures the inexplicable and therefore precious mystery of human life. Is this sanctity of an individual life an alien concept to those who do not believe in a divine origin or simply do not know if a divinity exists or how life itself was created?

Are we not bound therefore to respect the sanctity of life and individual conscience regardless of our theologies or lack thereof? Is this not a reasonable and obvious basis for regarding those sanctities as "unalienable"—beyond the authority of government to deny us? Is this not, then,

28 https://www.christianity.com/church/church-history/timeline/1501-1600/martin-luthers-most-noble-words-11629925.html

a sufficient basis for denying government the power to extend its authority over individual conscience and its expression, and to protect the individual from the tyranny of the state?

Luther regarded the community of believers as one formed by believers in the divinity of Christ. But the community of believers can also be founded on a shared reverence for the creation itself. For the miracle and mystery of human life. Or on acceptance of the principles enshrined in the Constitution and the Bill of Rights. Despite the obvious vast inequalities between individuals, do we not share a common humanity, which causes us to appreciate the fragility and preciousness of an individual life? Is this not a firm basis for treating each other with equal respect—with a religious regard for the integrity and independence of what a man of faith like Martin Luther would call our individual souls?

Because no one talks to God, religious values are basically attitudes that, over millennia, have been recognized as contributions to a better life: Gratitude, Reverence, Humility, Charity, Forgiveness, and Hope. Because religious attitudes are human commitments, perversions of a positive faith are common as well: bigotry, hate, and a desire to commit adversaries real and imagined to hellfire and damnation. But under Luther's influence, it is the positive values of a Christian faith that have been instituted in the constitutional framework of American law.

The Lutheran principles of a free society—religious or secular—can be summarized in three axioms: first, the equality of all before the law; second, the freedom of all in matters of conscience; and third, the unalienable nature of the rights protecting these two.

For Luther, the congregation of souls governed by these principles was confined to believers in the divinity of Christ. But the author of the Declaration of Independence, Thomas Jefferson, was a Deist who did not believe in the divinity of Christ. "I have ever thought religion a concern purely between our God and our consciences for which we were accountable to Him, and not to the priests."[29] These words express in American terms the core principles of Luther's Reformation.

The American founders secularized Luther's principles. The Protestant Christians who settled and created America were refugees from religious persecution by churches commanding the power of the state. Luther's Reformation created a diversity of Protestant denominations, and this diversity precluded the marriage of Church and State. Henceforth, there would be no one "true" religion.

To prevent one American church from becoming a religion established by the state, the Founders instituted a secular government and created a foundational right to the freedom of religious conscience and expression. Though no one articulated it as such, the American

29 https://founders.archives.gov/documents/Jefferson/03-10-02-0186

Founders could be said to have modified Luther's rights of Christian believers to rights of believers in the principles of the Declaration and the Constitution. In Jefferson's Deist formulation they were granted unalienable rights by a power beyond human interventions—by "Nature's God."[30]

It is a formulation surely acceptable to any agnostic or reasonable atheist who no more understands the mysteries of creation than does anyone else. The Lutheran principles, which once applied only to the community of Christian believers, were thus extended by the diversity of sects created by Luther's Reformation, to a universal community of believers in the values embraced by the Founders and derived from Luther's creed.

Slavery—A Flaw in the American Design

The American colonies inherited a system of economic slavery from the British that violated every precept of the liberties they granted to free citizens. Slaves were not included in their proclamation that every soul had a God-given, unalienable right to liberty. But the inclusion of slaves was in their hearts. In 1779, Jefferson, who was himself a slaveowner, proposed a law designed to lead to

---

30 https://constitutingamerica.org/90day-dcin-laws-of-nature-and-of-natures
-god-and-the-american-declaration-of-independence-guest-essayist-tony
-williams/

the emancipation of all slaves. The law was blocked by the slaveholding South. There were other such proposals that failed. Nonetheless, within twenty years of the American founding, slavery was abolished in the northern states,[31] and the slave trade was outlawed in North America. It remained a legal institution only in the South, whose economy was based on a plantation system sustained by human chattel.

In assessing the rationale for this hypocrisy, it is important to recognize that America's plantation system in tobacco and cotton was not only a source of individual wealth but of national strength, and specifically military strength. This strength was crucial to supporting America's independence—and freedoms—against slave-owning colonial powers like Protestant England and Catholic Spain. Consequently, even though it was a clear and embarrassing contradiction to their revolutionary aspirations, Americans didn't face a simple intellectual or moral choice when it came to ending the slave system. They faced the ruinous prospect of civil war.

The end of the slave trade in 1807 provides a marker with which to measure an underappreciated aspect of American slavery and the attacks it posthumously endured. Not only did America account for a minimal portion of the global slave trade—some 450,000 slaves out of 11.3 million in the Atlantic slave trade and 57

---

31 https://socialwelfare.library.vcu.edu/eras/colonial-postrev/act-to-prohibit-the-importation-of-slaves-1807/

million globally[32]—but it was a relatively benign form of this oppressive institution. Spanish and Portuguese slave systems in the Western hemisphere were so cruel in their methods that entire slave populations had to be replaced, often on an annual basis. But between 1807, when the United States outlawed the slave trade, and 1860—the eve of the Civil War—the slave population in America increased by natural means from one million to four million,[33] a reflection of the more humane conditions of what remained a vile institution. By the time of the Civil War there were five hundred thousand free Blacks in the United States,[34] about three thousand of whom were slaveowners themselves.[35]

Despite the claims of enemies of the American enterprise, "white supremacy" and racial oppression were not determing factors in Americans' failure to abolish slavery in 1776, 1787, or even in 1807, when the trade was outlawed. For three thousand years slavery was regarded as a normal institution in all societies. Yet, slavery has

---

32 https://www.aei.org/carpe-diem/thomas-sowell-on-slavery-and-this-fact-there-are-more-slaves-today-than-were-seized-from-africa-in-four-centuries/

33 https://www2.census.gov/library/publications/decennial/1850/1850c/1850c-04.pdf; https://www.njstatelib.org/research_library/new_jersey_resources/highlights/african_american_history_curriculum/unit_5_antebellum_america/

34 https://nationalhumanitiescenter.org/pds/maai/identity/text3/text3read.htm ; https://memory.loc.gov/ammem/aaohtml/exhibit/aopart2b.html; https://www.britannica.com/topic/African-American/Slavery-in-the-United-States

35 https://www.theroot.com/did-black-people-own-slaves-1790895436

been absurdly called "America's original sin."[36] In point
of historical fact, America not only accounted for a minis-
cule fraction of the global slave trade, but slavery existed
in Africa for a thousand years before a white man—let
alone an American—set foot there. Slavery still exists in
Black and Muslim Africa today.

In its three-thousand-year existence prior to the
American revolution, no one declared slavery "immoral"—
not Moses, not Jesus, and certainly not Mohammed—
until William Wilberforce, a white, Christian Englishman,
and his followers did at the end of the eighteenth century. Wilberforce was followed by Thomas Jefferson, who
declared slavery a violation of God's law in the Declaration
of Independence, setting the stage for a world-shaking
revolution, led by Britain, France, and the US that would
abolish the institution in the Western Hemisphere and
throughout the British and French Empires.

If racism was the cause of American slavery, how could
America be the home of five hundred thousand free Blacks
on the eve of the Civil War? The historical reality is that
tribal Black Africa had a product to sell—Black African
slaves—and Europeans were willing to profit from the
sale. But the majority of the Protestant Christian founders of America were committed to the principles of equality and freedom, and, at great cost, eventually prevailed.

---

36 https://www.foreignaffairs.com/articles/united-states/2017-12-12/americas
   -original-sin

The Civil War over America's Identity

The actual attitude of America's revolutionary leaders towards slavery was eloquently summarized by James Madison, the chief architect of the Constitution, as "the most oppressive dominion ever exercised by man over man."[37] Like Madison, Thomas Jefferson, to whose Declaration every emancipated descendant of slaves owes their freedom, was also an owner of slaves, trapped in circumstances he could not see his way past. In a passage of the Declaration, which did not make its way into the final version because of the objections of the southern colonies, Jefferson wrote this indictment of the British King:

> He has waged cruel war against human nature itself, violating its most sacred rights of life and liberty in the persons of a distant people who never offended him, captivating & carrying them into slavery in another hemisphere or to incur miserable death in their transportation thither.[38]

Years later Jefferson wondered:

> Can the liberties of a nation be thought to be secure when we have removed their only firm basis, a conviction in the minds of the people that these liberties are a

---

37 https://avalon.law.yale.edu/18th_century/debates_606.asp

38 https://www.thehenryford.org/explore/blog/the-deleted-slavery-passage-from
-the-declaration-of-independence

gift from God? That they are not to be violated but with His wrath? . . . I tremble for my country when I reflect that God is just and that his justice cannot sleep forever.[39]

Pause for a moment to reflect on this Jeffersonian nightmare. First, the recognition that slavery—however abhorrent to enlightened humanity—was nonetheless a perversely human norm. Even after slavery ceased to be a viable form of economic order, who would deny that the dominion of man over man is the human norm and liberty the exception? Jefferson was rightly concerned that unless people saw liberty as "a gift from God," there was no defending it. Left to the whims and inclinations of men of all races and creeds, coercion and dominion would be the rule. Thus, the prominent role of collectivist tyrannies in recent history can only be explained by this propensity of human beings to control and oppress their fellows.

A hundred and fifty years after the Emancipation Proclamation, radical enemies of America's democracy seek to deny the nation's role as a pioneer of freedom. They recast its historical legacy, falsely portraying it as "white supremacist" and "racist" from its inception. In a historical fiction as malicious as the *Protocols of the Elders of Zion*, the editorial board of the *New York Times*—the voice of America's cultural elites—claimed in 2020 that

---

39 Jefferson, *Notes on the State of Virginia*.; https://books.google.com /books?id=D6BQmzKvajIC&pg=PA149&lpg=#v=onepage&q&f=false ; https://www.tuscaloosanews.com/story/news/2001/09/03/madison-quote -misused/27811386007/; https://trib.com/opinion/letters/more-than-a -philosopher/article_0a354646-90a6-5058-aa47-a944ef59278c.html

America's founding was not 1776 but 1619, an obvious absurdity. According to the "1619 Project," America's founding was a date marked not by a manifesto of freedom but by the introduction of twenty African slaves into the Virginia Colony.[40]

In point of historical fact, the twenty were not slaves but indentured servants, scheduled to be freed after five to seven years of service to pay for their passage. At the time, the majority of the Virginia labor force was composed of indentured servants, and all but these twenty were white.[41] Driven by their hate and undaunted by the facts, proponents of the 1619 thesis portray the arrival of these twenty Africans as "the beginning of American slavery."[42]

Far from conveying a historical insight, the 1619 Project is more accurately seen as the symbolic crucifixion of a nation, based on two brazen lies. The creation of America was actually more than a century away, while in 1619, and for many years thereafter, slavery did not exist in England's Virginia Colony.[43]

---

40 https://www.theguardian.com/us-news/2019/aug/14/slavery-in-america-1619-first-ships-jamestown

41 https://www.pbs.org/opb/historydetectives/feature/indentured-servants-in-the-us/; https://www.history.com/this-day-in-history/first-african-slave-ship-arrives-jamestown-colony

42 https://www.nytimes.com/interactive/2019/08/14/magazine/1619-america-slavery.html

43 https://www.theguardian.com/us-news/2019/aug/14/slavery-in-america-1619-first-ships-jamestown: In this piece, the Black historian Nell Irvin Painter writes: "People were not enslaved in Virginia in 1619, they were indentured. The twenty or so Africans were sold and bought as 'servants' for a term of

The purpose of the poisonous 1619 Project was explained by the *New York Times* editors in these words: "In the days and weeks to come, we will publish essays demonstrating that nearly everything that has made America exceptional grew out of slavery."[44] A psychological warfare unit for America's most determined enemy could not have come up with a more malicious slander. But thanks to the domination of American educational institutions by the anti-American Left, these attempts to stand American history on its head and turn the nation's virtues into vices was immediately introduced as a curriculum into thousands of American public schools.[45]

The grotesque caricature promoted by the *Times*, the Pulitzer Foundation, and America's elites was generally worthy of America's collectivist enemies Communists, fascists, and Islamic jihadists. It was the furthest cry from the hymn to America's inspirational founding contained in Lincoln's Gettysburg address, which memorialized the fallen Union soldiers who gave their lives to end slavery, and described America as "a nation conceived in liberty and dedicated to the proposition that all men are created equal." The Civil War was a test, Lincoln declared, "to see whether that nation, or any nation so conceived and so

---

years, and they joined a population consisting largely of European indentured servants, mainly poor people from the British Isles whom the Virginia Company of London had transported and sold into servitude."

44 https://amgreatness.com/2019/08/16/the-mountebank-left-is-banking-on-you/

45 https://dc.medill.northwestern.edu/blog/2020/07/21/the-1619-project
-curriculum-taught-in-over-4500-schools-frederick-county-public-schools-has
-the-option/#sthash.Hpw9iAxz.dpbs

dedicated, can long endure."[46] It was a war that by its end would claim the sacrifice of more American lives than all America's wars into the present combined.[47]

In their bid to obliterate America and its founding, America's domestic enemies ignore these sacrifices and the complex motives of those who made them. They damn both parties to the Civil War, and Lincoln himself, as "white supremacists and racists."[48] These attitudes have no historical basis in fact. They are the malignant fantasies of haters of the American dream.

So resistant was humanity at large to ending slavery that, following the Civil War, it took more than sixty years to roll back slavery globally, and then incompletely. The costly effort to end the slave trade was the work of white western civilizations all imbued with the doctrines of Christianity and the Enlightenment, and powered by their industrial capitalist economies.

Led by the British Crown and the British navy, white Europeans and Americans proceeded to force the end of the slave trade throughout the empires they had created. They were opposed by non-white local authorities, African kings who were also slavers, but chiefly by the non-white Ottoman empire, whose Muslim traders were particularly sadistic, slitting the throats of African slaves

---

46 https://www.abrahamlincolnonline.org/lincoln/speeches/gettysburg.htm

47 https://www.statista.com/statistics/1009819/total-us-military-fatalities-in
    -american-wars-1775-present/

48 E.g., Lerone Bennett, *Forced Into Glory: Abraham Lincoln's White Dream*,
    2000. https://en.wikipedia.org/wiki/Forced_into_Glory

when their boats were intercepted and casting them over-board to drown rather than go free.[49]

The Racist Counter-Revolution

In America, anti-Black racism first reared its head in a major way in the struggles that led to the Civil War, and then into the post-emancipation, segregated future in the South. Ironically, this development was the product of the very egalitarian creed enshrined in the Declaration of Independence. When the Declaration was signed in 1776, it marked the beginning of an eighty-four-year cold war between pro-slavery and pro-freedom Americans. This war was only resolved through an explosion of violence that killed more Americans than all of America's previous and future wars. The victory of the forces of equality and freedom was sealed with the Emancipation Proclamation and the 13th, 14th and 15th Amendments, which abolished slavery in the United States of America for good.

Throughout the eighty-four-year conflict, leaders on both sides recognized that their opponents posed an existential threat. Speaking for free America in his "House Divided" speech, Lincoln summarized their fears in these words:

Either the opponents of slavery will arrest the further spread of it, and place it where the public mind shall

---

49 https://www.youtube.com/watch?v=IRiKFjhlEcQ

rest in the belief that it is in the course of ultimate extinction, or its advocates will push it forward, till it shall become alike lawful in all the states, old as well as new—North as well as South.[50]

A leading spokesman for the slave South, George Fitzhugh, also predicted that "one set of ideas will govern and control after a while the civilized world. Slavery will everywhere be abolished, or everywhere re-instituted."[51]

While regional issues provided obvious bases for the Civil War, the heart of the conflict was between two political factions, with two incompatible views of the nature of the Union which joined them. In Lincoln's words,

> the Republican Party . . . hold that this government was instituted to secure the blessings of freedom, and that slavery is an unqualified evil to the Negro, to the white man, to the soil and to the State . . . They will use every constitutional method to prevent the evil from becoming larger and . . . will oppose, in all its length and breadth, the modern Democratic idea, that slavery is as good as freedom, and ought to have room for expansion all over the continent.[52]

Within seventy-four years of America's formal creation in 1787, anti-slavery Americans, led by their president, engaged in a war and made the ultimate sacrifice to ensure

---

50 https://www.nps.gov/liho/learn/historyculture/housedivided.htm

51 https://muse.jhu.edu/book/72307/pdf

52 https://quod.lib.umich.edu/l/lincoln/lincoln3/1:13?rgn=div1;view=fulltext

that the vile institution was abolished, and America's slaves were set free.

Until the issue was resolved by war, America's young history was dominated by this conflict. While contested, America's founding vision of liberty and equality as unalienable human rights was so contagious that the anti-slavery movement it inspired steadily gathered momentum through the years. As Dinesh D'Souza states in his invaluable work on this American past:

> After the Revolution there was a big change. By 1804 every state north of Maryland had abolished slavery, either immediately or gradually. Thus, by the end of the founding era, more than a hundred thousand slaves had been freed—around one-sixth of the total number in the country at the time—and slavery was gone, or on its way out, in seven of the thirteen original states.[53]

The anti-slavery sentiment, now a prominent theme of free Americans, was reflected in the advocacies of George Mason, a Virginia planter who had a major influence on the Constitution despite his refusal to sign it. His objections were that the document lacked a Bill of Rights and failed to outlaw the slave trade. Speaking in July 1773 at the Virginia Constitutional Convention, he described slavery as "that slow Poison, which is daily contaminating

53 D'Souza, Dinesh. *Death of a Nation* (pp. 46-47). Kindle Edition; https://books.google.com/books?id=VOw7DwAAQBAJ&pg=PT37&lpg=#v=onepage&q&f=false

the Minds and Morals of our People."[54] Despite the ominous tone of his concern, his anti-slavery views were destined to prevail.

The call to freedom flourished not only in the North but in the South as well. In 1787, Southern states joined Northern states in excluding slavery from the Northwest Territory and—twenty years later—in abolishing the African slave trade. As John Blassingame, an African American historian of slavery noted, "Many planters convinced of the immorality of bondage joined with clergymen in seeking its abolition." So powerful were the anti-slavery currents even in the South that the region supported more than a hundred antislavery organizations, and manumissions of slaves were fairly common.[55]

To counter this movement, the planters mounted a historically unprecedented campaign to defend the institution. One line of defense was their opposition to the industrial capitalism of the North, whose practices they compared unfavorably to the slave system. George Fitzhugh, a socialist and one of slavery's chief defenders wrote: "Socialism proposes to do away with free competition; to afford protection and support at all times to

---

54 https://www.fairfaxtimes.com/arts_entertainment/revolutionary-history
-lives-at-gunston-hall/article_d0f06e78-5b9e-11ed-9a97-63e026a27a44.html
; https://www.post-gazette.com/news/portfolio/2006/03/28/Founding-father
-makes-the-Final-Four/stories/200603280162 ; https://books.google.com
/books?id=VOw7DwAAQBAJ&pg=PT41&lpg=#v=onepage&q&f=false

55 https://books.google.com/books?id=VOw7DwAAQBAJ&pg=PT41
&lpg=#v=onepage&q&f=false

the laboring class . . . these purposes, slavery fully and perfectly attains."[56]

But the main conundrum for the pro-slavery argument, whose advocates considered themselves patriots, was the proclamation contained in America's founding document that "all men are created equal and are endowed by their Creator with an unalienable right to . . . liberty." This creed was clearly incompatible with slavery and became a focus of the pro-slavery counterattack. Its leading spokesmen recognized the existential nature of its threat and responded by rejecting this most fundamental American creed. Senator John C. Calhoun, a leading spokesman for the slave-owning class, minced no words, calling Jefferson's self-evident truths "an utterly false view of the subordinate relation of the Black to the white race."[57] The alleged inequality of the races soon became a clarion call of the South's rebellion against the American social contract, forming the basis for the South's secession, and also for the segregationist creed that followed its loss of the war.

On the outbreak of the Civil War, Alexander Stephens, vice-president of the newly formed Confederacy, explained how this conflict over the American founding lay at the heart of the war itself:

> Jefferson in his forecast, had anticipated this [conflict], as the 'rock upon which the old Union would split.' He was

---

56 https://mises.org/wire/george-fitzhugh-honest-socialist

57 https://kdhist.sitehost.iu.edu/H105-documents-web/week13 /CalhounreOregon1848.html

right. What was conjecture with him, is now a realized fact. But whether he fully comprehended the great truth upon which that rock stood and stands, may be doubted. The prevailing ideas entertained by him and most of the leading statesmen at the time of the formation of the old constitution, were that the enslavement of the African was in violation of the laws of nature; that it was wrong in principle, socially, morally, and politically. . . .

Those ideas, however, were fundamentally wrong. They rested upon the assumption of the equality of races. This was an error. It was a sandy foundation, and the government built upon it fell when the 'storm came and the wind blew.' Our new [Confederate] government is founded upon exactly the opposite idea; its foundations are laid, its cornerstone rests, upon the great truth that the negro is not equal to the white man; that slavery subordination to the superior race is his natural and normal condition. This, our new government, is the first, in the history of the world, based upon this great physical, philosophical, and moral truth.[58]

The Second Civil War

The victory of the free North and the demise of the Confederacy in the Civil War did not lead to a reconciliation over what had become the central issue of the

---

58 https://www.theatlantic.com/entertainment/archive/2011/05/in-defense-of
-slavery/239719/; https://www.ucl.ac.uk/USHistory/Building/docs
/Cornerstone.htm

conflict—race. On the contrary, out of the wounds of war, a virulent strain of racism rose in the defeated South to assert the justice of the cause that had been lost on the battlefield. Stripped of their armies, southerners set about implementing a social reconstruction designed to institutionalize the slaveowners' racist view of human nature and justify their losing cause.

Before he was assassinated, Lincoln sponsored the so-called "Reconstruction Amendments" to the Constitution,[59] which recognized the full equality of the African slaves he had liberated, according them the same rights as free Americans. But Lincoln's assassination brought to power a southern politician and Democrat who did not share his anti-slavery or Christian passions. President Andrew Johnson nullified these rights without formally repealing them, and empowered the leaders of the defeated South to implement their own reconstruction—a segregation of the races designed to institutionalize and make permanent the inferior status of America's Black citizens, and thus to justify the pro-slavery cause in the war they had lost.

The segregation of freed Blacks in the American south began with the infamous Black Codes and the denial of Blacks' right to vote. Like other racist restrictions on the recently liberated slaves, this denial was enforced by a generalized reign of terror in the South. On May 1, 1866, in Memphis, for example, shots were fired between white

---

59 https://www.studentsofhistory.com/the-reconstruction-amendments

policemen and Black veterans recently mustered out of the Union Army. Afterwards, "mobs of white residents and policemen rampaged through Black neighborhoods and the houses of freedmen, attacking and killing Black soldiers and civilians and committing many acts of robbery and arson."[60]

A subsequent report by a joint Congressional Committee detailed the carnage, with Blacks suffering most of the injuries and deaths by far: 46 Black and 2 white people were killed, 75 Black people injured, over 100 Black persons robbed, 5 Black women raped, and 91 homes, 4 churches, and 8 schools (every Black church and school) burned in the Black community. Modern estimates place property losses at over $100,000, suffered mostly by Black people. Many Black people fled the city permanently; by 1870, their population had fallen by one quarter compared to 1865."[61]

Similar racial massacres took place periodically to keep Black citizens in place and to shore up the systemic segregation that established Black inferiority and white supremacy in every significant aspect of social life. Marriage between whites and Blacks were banned. "Signs were used to show non-Whites where they could legally walk, talk, drink, rest, or eat. For those places that were

---

60 https://americansall.org/legacy-story-group/jim-crow-violence-examples
   -race-riots-and-lynchings-1866-1898

61 United States Congress, House Select Committee on the Memphis Riots,
   Memphis Riots and Massacres, 25 July 1866, Washington, DC: Government
   Printing Office (reprinted by Arno Press, Inc., 1969)

racially mixed, Blacks had to wait until all White cus-
tomers were dealt with. Rules were also enforced that
restricted African Americans from entering white stores.
Segregated facilities extended from white-only schools to
white-only graveyards."[62] While these "Jim Crow" laws
were generally confined to the South, the racist presidency
of Woodrow Wilson saw them extended to the federal
government. This federal segregation lasted until the end
of World War II, a conflict in which Black and white troops
fought in segregated units that were unequally supplied.

Directly after the Civil War ended, terrorist groups
began to appear in the South to enforce the segregated
caste system and intimidate free Blacks and proponents
of equal rights from fighting back. Most prominent and
powerful among these groups was the white supremacist
Ku Klux Klan. Founded by former Confederate gener-
als, the Klan conducted cross burnings, random murders,
lynchings, and other acts of violence to strike fear into the
hearts of anyone resisting the caste system. A low point of
the nation's support for this racist plague was Woodrow
Wilson's decision to screen *Birth of a Nation* at the White
House. Based on the KKK novel *The Clansman*, the film
demonized Blacks, celebrated the Klan, and promoted its
white supremacist agenda.

With Woodrow Wilson's imprimatur, the Klan became
a major political force, encompassing an estimated 4–6

62 https://www.blackfacts.com/fact/racial-segregation-in-the-united
-states; https://www.youtube.com/watch?v=cL4ypwW5SMY

million members at its height. "By the end of the [1920s]," reported the *Washington Post*, "the organization, whose membership remained semi-secret, claimed 11 governors, 16 senators and as many as 75 congressmen."[63] This gave the Klan enough political muscle through the Democrat Party to legitimize the segregationist system in the South for the next two generations.

A Civil Rights Revolution

The attacks on freedmen inspired a movement in Black America to form communal institutions and to adopt ways and attitudes that refuted the negative stereotypes racists were using to stigmatize them as inferior. This movement identified itself as a campaign to create a "New Negro"— middle-class, conservative, and educated.

Education had been denied to the slaves. Consequently, among the most important institutions supporting this movement were Black schools of higher learning known as Historically Black Colleges and Universities (HBCUs). The first of these, Cheney University, was created in 1837 in Pennsylvania to serve freed Blacks. It was created by a donation from a white Quaker who was an abolitionist.[64]

---

63 https://www.washingtonpost.com/news/made-by-history/wp/2018/03/15/how-social-media-spread-a-historical-lie/

64 https://cheyney.edu/who-we-are/the-first-hbcu/

Many more HBCUs were created in the Reconstruction era and were funded by the federal government.

Thanks to these developments, a new civil rights movement emerged in the South, as the twentieth century began. It was led by the National Association for the Advancement of Colored People (NAACP) created in 1909. Like the movement itself, the NAACP was the product of a coalition of whites and Blacks. The first president of the NAACP, Moorfield Storey, was white. He served as its president from its inception in 1909 for its first twenty years until his death in 1929.[65] The highest NAACP award, the Spingarn Medal, is named after a Jew who played a leading role in the organization and served as its president from 1930 to 1939.[66] Led by the NAACP, the civil rights movement engaged in legal battles to provide voting rights to Blacks, enforce the Reconstruction Amendments, and create anti-lynching legislation which the segregationists were able to block.

Black Nationalism, Black Supremacy

Unfortunately, historical processes are not so simple as to provide neat solutions to the conflicts they create. Along with the resistance to southern racism mounted by the integrationists, who sought to restore—or complete—the

---

65 https://www.harvardmagazine.com/2018/07/moorfield-storey
66 https://rhapsodyinbooks.wordpress.com/2009/06/29/june-29-1914
-the-spingarn-medal-was-established-by-the-naacp/

vision of the American founding, movements arose in the
Black community that did not believe an inclusive and
egalitarian solution to the problem was either feasible or
desirable. Instead, they reproduced the tribalism of the
white supremacists in reverse, proposing a race war on
the one hand and a racial exodus on the other, as the only
viable solutions to the problem.

The exodus solution was the brainchild of a Black
nationalist and racist named Marcus Garvey, a Jamaican
who emigrated to the United States in 1916. Garvey
was a Pan-Africanist who declared himself "Provisional
President of Africa" and believed that Africans should
be reunited with their racial brothers and sisters who
had been dispersed across the oceans by the slave trade.
Garvey was a racial purist and separatist, prompting
him to form alliances with the KKK, which had similar views.[67] Though never as influential as the NAACP,
Garvey's movement claimed to have two million members
and chapters in twenty-five states.[68] Ultimately, Garvey's
criminal behaviors and personal indiscretions limited his
otherwise formidable impact.

A more powerful and influential movement was the
Nation of Islam, whose Black supremacist creed was
the invention of its founder, Wallace Fard Muhammad.
According to Nation doctrine, Allah, who is Black, created

---

67 https://www.archives.gov/research/african-americans/individuals/marcus
    -garvey
68 https://maap.columbia.edu/mbl_place/49.html; https://www.historydaily.com
    /black-nationalist-marcus-garvey-goes-to-prison/

the first humans, the dark-skinned Tribe of Shabazz. A scientist named Yakub then created whites by diluting Black blood, thereby creating an inferior race. The whites were intrinsically violent. They overthrew the Tribe of Shabazz and achieved global dominance. The Nation of Islam calls for the creation of an independent Black nation state within the territorial United States. It claims that Wallace Fard Muhammad, who died or disappeared in 1934, will return aboard a spaceship to wipe out the white race.[69]

What these movements did was give license to Blacks to become aggressors in the racial wars and, in the process, adopt the hatreds, bigotries, and genocidal agendas of their worst enemies. These attitudes were soon to result in the defeat of the greatest attempt to complete the American revolution and realize its promise of equality and inclusion for all.

An American Solution

In the year that Wallace Fard Muhammad disappeared, a Baptist minister named Michael King made a pilgrimage to Jerusalem and then to Europe, where he attended an international religious conference in Germany. At the conference, he learned about the remarkable life and teachings of Martin Luther, which so impressed him that

---

69 https://www.discoverthenetworks.org/organizations/nation-of-islam-noi
/; https://www.adl.org/resources/profile/nation-islam; https://www
.discoverthenetworks.org/individuals/wallace-fard-muhammad/

he changed his own name to Martin Luther King and that of his young son to Martin Luther King Jr.

The young King was educated at Moorhouse College, an HBCU, and at Boston University, which, like most schools outside the South, was integrated. In his thirties, he became one of America's great orators and the spiritual leader of a triumphant civil rights movement. Martin Luther King Jr. shared his revolutionary namesake's foundational belief that the individual's conscience is sacrosanct—"captive to the word of God"—and therefore beyond the reach of the state. "To deprive man of freedom," King wrote in his autobiography," is to relegate him to the status of a thing, rather than elevate him to the status of a person. Man must never be treated as a means to the end of the state, but always as an end within himself."[70]

King was a disciple of Mahatma Gandhi, committed to non-violence as a political strategy, which served to win his efforts widespread respect. The high point of his political career came in 1963 during a civil rights "March on Washington," where he addressed over a quarter of a million followers, Black and white, giving what is per-haps the second most famous speech in American history after Lincoln's Gettysburg Address. Its crowning passage summed up the distinctive American spirit of equality and pluralism in these words:

---

70 https://www.aei.org/carpe-diem/quotation-of-the-day-ii-on-the-evils-of
    -communism/

I still have a dream. It is a dream deeply rooted in the American dream. I have a dream that one day this nation will rise up and live out the true meaning of its creed. We hold these truths to be self-evident that all men are created equal.

I have a dream that one day out in the red hills of Georgia the sons of former slaves and the sons of former slaveowners will be able to sit down together at the table of brotherhood.

I have a dream that one day even the state of Mississippi, a state sweltering with the heat of oppression, will be transformed into an oasis of freedom and justice.

I have a dream that my four little children will one day live in a nation where they will not be judged by the color of their skin but by the content of their character.[71]

The following year, Congress passed the Civil Rights Act outlawing systemic racism, creating—actually re-enforcing—the legal framework for this American vision. King's achievement was recognized in the award of the Nobel Peace Prize in 1965. The centrality of his crusade to the American project was recognized in 1983, when President Ronald Reagan signed a bill that created a national holiday in his honor.[72] King remains the only individual so honored.

---

71 https://www.npr.org/2010/01/18/122701268/i-have-a-dream-speech-in-its
    -entirety

72 https://www.politico.com/story/2017/11/02/reagan-establishes-national
    -holiday-for-mlk-nov-2-1983-244328

While King provided the moral inspiration for Americans to implement the vision of America's founders, the nation's attitudes towards race had already changed by the time King's movement was formed during the Montgomery Bus boycott in the mid-1950s.[73] A powerful impetus for the change was World War II. Having fought and defeated an enemy dedicated to establishing the rule of a "master race," Americans could no longer countenance the racism in their midst.

In 1947, Jackie Robinson broke the color bar in America's national sport. The following year, President Truman issued an executive order banning discrimination in the armed forces and in federal employment. In 1954, a landmark Supreme Court case integrated the nation's schools.[74] These were just markers of the unprecedented social revolution that was taking place in the United States. As of 2009, for example, there were nineteen times the number of Black American editors and reporters as there were in 1950, and thirty-three times as many Black engineers. As Stephan and Abigail Thernstrom report in *America in Black and White*: "In 1949, no sizeable city in the entire country had a Black mayor, and just two African Americans were members of Congress. [But by 2009] most of our largest cities have—or have had—a

73 https://www.history.com/topics/black-history/montgomery-bus-boycott
74 https://www.archives.gov/milestone-documents/brown-v-board-of-education#

Black chief executive, and more than forty Blacks hold seats in the House of Representatives."[75]

Of even greater national significance, in 2008 Americans elected their first Black president, Barack Obama, who prevailed in the election with 43 percent of the white vote,[76] truly a milestone in the two hundred-year effort by Americans to create an inclusive society.

Approval of interracial marriage is an index for anthropologists of how tolerant and inclusive diverse societies are. In 1958, barely 5 percent of Americans approved of interracial marriage. By 2007, the figure was almost 80 percent. The disapproval rate of Blacks (18 percent) exceeded that of whites (17 percent) although the difference was negligible.[77]

During these transformations, ordinary people generally failed to appreciate the dramatic advances that had been made. "In a 1991 Gallup poll, about one-fifth of all whites, but almost half of the Black respondents, indicated that they believed that at least three out of four African Americans—75 percent—were poor and lived in inner cities. In reality, according to federal poverty statistics, less

75 Stephan and Abigail Thernstrom, *America in Black and White*, 1999, Kindle Edition, p. 183.

76 https://www.politico.com/story/2008/11/exit-polls-how-obama-won-015297

77 https://en.wikipedia.org/wiki/Interracial_marriage_in_the_United_States, see the section on "Public Opinion"

than one-fifth of the African American population then consisted of impoverished residents of central cities."[78]

In retrospect, it is clear that King's "I Have a Dream" speech and the passage of the Civil Rights Act marked a historic moment when Americans signaled they were ready to fulfill the promise that America's founders had made in Philadelphia, nearly two hundred years earlier: to create a constitutional order that would grant equal rights before the law to all American citizens—a secular vision of equality parallel to the "priesthood of all believers" that had been advanced for the Christian world by Martin Luther.

A Tribal Counter-Revolution

Unfortunately, before this vision could be realized, tribal instincts asserted themselves within the heart of the civil rights movement, creating attitudes and forces that threatened the progress that had been made, and at the political level worked to reverse it.

In 1966, radicals in the civil rights coalition, who were grouped around the Student Non-Violent Coordinating Committee,[79] challenged King's leadership and values. They dropped the phrase "Non-Violent" from their

---

78 Thernstrom, op. cit., pp. 183-4.

79 https://www.discoverthenetworks.org/organizations/student-nonviolent
-coordinating-committee-sncc/

organizational charter and rejected King's ecumenical approach, insisting on the slogan "Black Power!"—a phrase designed to convey both racial hostility and a thinly veiled threat of violence. To emphasize his racial animus, their leader, Stokely Carmichael,[80] an immigrant from Trinidad, expelled all whites from the organization. "I've never admired a white man," he said provocatively, "but the greatest of them, to my mind, was Hitler."[81]

To underscore that he no longer considered himself a member of the American enterprise, Carmichael changed his name to "Kwame Ture" and, in 1969, exiled himself to Marxist Guinea, where he served as an aide to its ruthless dictator, Sekou Toure, who killed an estimated fifty thousand of its inhabitants before his death in 1984.[82] Carmichael-Ture periodically returned to the United States to speak. He also continued to cultivate his longstanding alliance and friendship with Nation of Islam leader Louis Farrakhan. Eventually, in 1996, Carmichael came to the United States to get medical treatment and accept accolades from his admirers before returning to Guinea, where he died in November 1998.[83]

---

80 https://www.discoverthenetworks.org/individuals/stokely-carmichael-aka -kwame-ture/

81 https://www.jewishpress.com/blogs/sultan-knish/sen-cory-booker-and-the -only-good-zionist-is-a-dead- zionist/2018/09/20/

82 https://jfk.artifacts.archives.gov/people/1827/president-sekou-toure?ctx=7126 2622c91d494e1e0306061042597e1d66f1ad&idx=17

83 https://www.deseret.com/1998/11/17/19412596/remembering-stokely -carmichael; https://www.youtube.com/watch?v=Q1C_bLJuNlo; https ://americanradioworks.publicradio.org/features/blackspeech/scarmichael .html; https://www.biography.com/activists/stokely-carmichael; https://www

In addition to being a racist and pro-Castro Marxist, Carmichael was a vocal anti-Semite. When the Arabs launched an unprovoked war on Israel in June 1967, its express purpose was the destruction of the Jewish state and the ethnic cleansing of its Jews. Carmichael's response was to align the civil rights cause with the Arab aggressors, infamously saying "The only good Zionist is a dead Zionist."[84]

This was a particularly savage and destructive attack since in the words of Jonathan Kaufman, an authority of the subject:

The cooperation of Blacks and Jews in the early 1960s set the standard for the great coalition that became the civil rights movement. At the height of that movement, three-quarters of the money raised by the Reverend Martin Luther King, Jr. and other civil rights leaders was donated by Jews. . . . During Freedom Summer of 1964, two thirds of the whites who went to the South to help Blacks to register and vote were Jews including Michael Schwerner and Andrew Goodman, murdered by white racists that summer along with Black civil rights worker James Earl Chaney.[85]

.washingtonpost.com/archive/lifestyle/1998/04/08/the-undying-revolutionary-as-stokely-carmichael-he-fought-for-black-power-now-kwame-tures-fighting-for-his-life/4adb14ec-0db8-4668-8af6-84f877b3c61a/

84 https://www.nytimes.com/1996/03/11/opinion/l-black-activist-disparages-jews-063096.html

85 Jonathan Kaufman, *Broken Alliance*, 1995, p. xi; https://books.google.com/books?id=1m--hIat1-YC&pg=PR11&lpg=PR11&dq=#v=onepage&q&f=false

The actions of the Carmichael militants divided and weakened King's civil rights coalition, and caused the NAACP and the National Urban League to leave its ranks.[86] However, fifty years later, Black Democrats like Senator Cory Booker were still invoking Carmichael as an American hero: "Stokely Carmichael said it best: we are the leaders we've been looking for."[87] Both Carmichael and Booker, and their many political allies, now attacked the Constitution itself as "racist" and "sexist," prefiguring the infamous 1619 Project embraced by the Biden White House.[88]

Following King's death by an assassin's hand in 1968, the leadership of King's civil rights cause fell to race hustlers like Jesse Jackson and Al Sharpton, as the NAACP and other civil rights organizations succumbed to the tribal influences of the political Left. Under the demagogic influence of Sharpton and Jackson, civil rights became a pretext for racial extortion.[89] Businesses were threatened with race-baiting boycotts unless they paid Sharpton's and Jackson's organizations ransom. Civil rights advocates revived the reparations claims that civil

86 https://timesmachine.nytimes.com/timesmachine/1967/06/30/83129131.html?pageNumber=15

87 https://www.jewishpress.com/blogs/sultan-knish/sen-cory-booker-and-the-only-good-zionist-is-a-dead-zionist/2018/09/20/

88 Ibid.

89 Kenneth R. Timmerman, *Shakedown: Exposing the Real Jesse Jackson*, 2002, https://www.amazon.com/Shakedown-Exposing-Real-Jesse-Jackson/dp/0895261650/ref=tmm_hrd_swatch_0?_encoding=UTF8&qid=1648484122&sr=8-1

rights leaders had previously rejected as divisive and
unnecessary. The Sharpton-Jackson tactics were also used
to extort concessions and racial privileges from educational and philanthropic organizations. Under the pressure of this new "civil rights" coalition, in the 1978 Bakke
Case, the Supreme Court declared institutional racism in
the form of "Affirmative Action" constitutional.[90]

In 1994, the radicals went an unconscionable step
further and welcomed into the civil rights coalition the
nation's most virulent racist and raving anti-Semite, Louis
Farrakhan,[91] who was also the leader of the nation's larg-
est Black supremacist organization. This surrender to
Black racism took place at the behest of a transformed
NAACP whose leaders invited Farrakhan to their 1994
"Summit."[92]

The invitation sparked protests, particularly
from Jewish groups because the previous November,
Farrakhan's chief spokesman, Khalid Abdul Muhammad,
had given a speech at a New Jersey College in which he
called Jews "bloodsuckers of the Black nation,"[93] a term
Farrakhan himself had used, accused them—falsely—of
owning 75 percent of the slaves, and of controlling the

90 https://www.oyez.org/cases/1979/76-811

91 https://www.discoverthenetworks.org/individuals/louis-farrakhan/#resources

92 https://www.nytimes.com/1994/02/20/us/naacp-invites-farrakhan.html

93 https://www.discoverthenetworks.org/individuals/khalid-abdul-muhammad
    /; https://www.nytimes.com/1994/02/28/nyregion/islamic-figure-in-new-tirade
    -against-jews.html; https://www.youtube.com/watch?v=E7MVbwVwrmI ;
    https://www.washingtonpost.com/archive/local/2001/02/18/khalid
    -muhammad-dies-at-53/ac0d1a96-b2d0-4a80-a1af-cee4c7c5f0e0/

government. Farrakhan endorsed Khalid's remarks but was not to be outdone in his hatred for the Jews: "I wonder, will you recognize Satan. I wonder if you will see the satanic Jew and the Synagogue of Satan . . because Satan has deceived the whole world."[94]

As previously noted, in Farrakhan's version of Islam, white people are by nature morally inferior to Blacks and a menace to humanity. Its doctrines prophecy that "a time of reckoning will soon arrive in which white people are finally overthrown in an apocalyptic race war, and dark-skinned Africans will once again reign supreme."[95]

Notwithstanding these repulsive views, "the NAACP"—as reported in the *New York Times*—"has recently tried to forge closer ties with the Nation of Islam, as have other prominent Blacks like Representative Kweisi Mfume, the Maryland Democrat who heads the Congressional Black Caucus; Representative Maxine Waters, Democrat of California; and the Rev. Jesse Jackson."[96] The NAACP's attitude in the face of the outrage its invitation inspired was expressed by its new chairman, William Gibson, who said, "The time has come again to come together."[97]

---

94 https://www.jpost.com/diaspora/louis-farrakhan-loses-twitter-verification
    -right-after-satanic-jew-rant-559738

95 https://study.com/academy/lesson/the-nation-of-islam-definition-beliefs-history
    .html#:~:text=The%20Nation%20of%20Islam%20believes,will%20
    once%20again%20reign%20supreme.

96 https://www.nytimes.com/1994/02/20/us/naacp-invites-farrakhan.html

97 https://greensboro.com/farrakhan-presence-protested-naacp-summit-tries-to
    -inspire-moral- renewal/article_d5607c6d-b1cd-56ce-b168-e6199ba2b3a6
    .html

There were dissenters. Julian Bond, a founder of the Student Non-Violent Coordinating Committee and former member of the Georgia House of representatives, was forthright in his rejection of the Summit: "[Farrakhan's] homophobia, anti-Semitism and retrograde racial separatism should make him an unwelcome guest at an NAACP-sponsored event," wrote Bond in the *Baltimore Sun*. "The NAACP's invitation to him makes it a partner in his hateful views of whites, Jews and homosexuals." For his part, Farrakhan was "happy and honored" to have been invited by "the oldest civil rights organization in this nation."[98]

The NAACP's embrace of Farrakhan was a measure of how far the civil rights cause had fallen, and how completely it had lost its moral compass. But the Summit was just a stepping stone in this descent, as Farrakhan announced his intention to hold a "Million Man March" in Washington DC, a transparent scheme to cloak himself and his malignant ravings in the mantle of King's historic march thirty-two years earlier. Farrakhan's ability to accomplish this feat was the direct result of his inclusion in the NAACP summit a year earlier.

On October 16, 1995, over four hundred thousand people gathered on the National Mall to honor the virulent racist. The march was organized by "The National African American Leadership Summit, the leading group

---

98 Ibid.

of civil rights activists and the Nation of Islam working with scores of civil rights organizations."[99]

Speakers included Farrakhan, who gave the keynote, Baraka Obama's America-hating pastor and confidant Jeremiah Wright,[100] Washington and Baltimore mayors Marion Berry and Kurt Schmoke, and the racist cult leader Maulana Karenga,[101] who invented Kwanzaa, a Black holiday to supplant Christmas. Karenga was the leader of an organization called United Slaves, recently released from prison where he had spent seven years for torturing two of his female disciples by inserting hot irons into their orifices. The march also featured familiar figures like Rosa Parks, Martin Luther King III, Maya Angelou,[102] and Cornel West.[103]

The Left's main criticism of the march was its emphasis on men, but at least one civil rights icon, John Lewis,[104] did not attend because, in his words, Farrakhan's message was to "resegregate America."[105]

Civil Rights had become a movement to divide Americans into racial groups, casting whites as the oppressors of everyone else, and portraying "people of color" as

99 https://www.history.com/this-day-in-history/million-man-march-1995

100 https://www.nationalreview.com/2008/05/left-church-stanley-kurtz/

101 https://thefederalist.com/2020/12/31/kwanzaa-is-a-fake-holiday-invented-by -a-criminal-marxist/

102 https://www.discoverthenetworks.org/individuals/maya-angelou/

103 https://www.influencewatch.org/person/cornel-west/

104 https://keywiki.org/John_Lewis

105 https://www.upi.com/Archives/1995/10/14/Opinions-differ-on-purpose-of -march/9981813643200/

victims with no responsibility for their circumstances in life. This, despite the fact that 80 percent of Blacks now lived above the poverty line.[106]

The Democrats' Racial Regression

The seeds of this shift to a new tribalism that defined and divided Americans by race had been sown a quarter of a century earlier, when the radical Left staged a riot at the Democrats' presidential convention. The riot was designed by its organizers to defeat the Democrats' anti-Communist presidential candidate, Hubert Humphrey, in the coming election. After the riot, leftists marched en masse into the party they had despised and created ethnic caucuses in the House to institutionalize their balkanized view of America. This development gave rise to a generation of politicians committed to tribal values and an anti-American radicalism well to the left of the majority of Black Americans, and indeed of all Americans.

Over the next fifty years the Democrat Party became the party of racial divisions, shaping its malicious campaigns to portray Republicans as heirs to Klan racism. Leading party figures such as Barack Obama, Bill Clinton, and Black Caucus head Kwesi Mfume cozied up to Farrakhan as though he didn't represent everything they

---

106 https://www.statista.com/statistics/205059/percentage-of-poor-black
    -families-in-the-us/

claimed to hate. Even though they had created the segregated system in the South and recently led the resistance to the 1964 Civil Rights Act,[107] Democrats brazenly posed as equal rights advocates. They did so while weaponizing race in their national and local campaigns, slandering as a "racist"—without exception—every Republican presidential candidate beginning with George H. W. Bush. Among other libels, their campaign messages regularly threatened that "Black churches would burn" if Republicans were elected.[108] When Barack Obama became president in 2008, criticisms of his left-wing politics were relentlessly dismissed by Democrats as expressions of anti-Black racism.

The ludicrous nature of these racial attacks was highlighted during the 2012 campaign when vice presidential candidate Joe Biden—recently a close friend of senatorial leaders of the Klan like Virginia senator Robert Byrd[109]—warned a mixed audience that if Republicans Mitt Romney and Paul Ryan were elected, "They're gonna put y'all back in chains."[110] But its extreme expression was the more recent attacks on the candidacy and then presidency of Donald Trump,

107 https://www.wsj.com/articles/SB1041302509432817073; https://www.dailysignal.com/2018/12/17/fact-check-more-republicans-voted-for-the-civil-rights-act-as-a-percentage-than-democrats-did/

108 https://www.foxnews.com/story/steele-responds-to-democrats-attacks-on-gop

109 https://www.discoverthenetworks.org/individuals/robert-byrd/

110 https://www.theatlantic.com/politics/archive/2012/08/joe-biden-threatens-republicans-will-put-you-chains/324728/

whom Democrats smeared as a "white nationalist" and "white supremacist."

These slanders were levelled against a man who had been a lifelong supporter of Democrats and their liberal causes, and in 1986 had received an NAACP award alongside Rosa Parks and Muhammad Ali, presented to them by Jesse Jackson.[111] It was also despite the fact that during the campaign and his presidency, Trump had made special outreaches to Black communities and added large federal contributions to Black institutions like Historically Black Colleges and Universities.[112]

Along with their malicious racial attacks on Trump and his supporters, the Democrat Party officially endorsed Black Lives Matter—a Marxist organization whose patron saint was a convicted Marxist cop-killer, Assata Shakur, now in exile in Communist Cuba. Black Lives Matter had orchestrated violent riots in 220 American cities in the summer of 2020, sowing hatred against America's law enforcement agencies by accusing them of wantonly killing unarmed Blacks for their skin color. It was a claim for which there was no evidence, and which no crime statistic supported.[113]

111 https://www.nytimes.com/1986/10/16/nyregion/80-named-as-recipients-of-ellis-island-awards.html

112 https://apnews.com/article/c4834e48841d97c5a93312b1bf75302a

113 David Horowitz, *I Can't Breathe: How A Racial Hoax Is Killing America*, Regnery 2021, pp. 152-156; https://www.discoverthenetworks.org/organizations/black-lives-matter-blm/

Black Lives Matter had come to national promi-
nence with the 2014 shooting death of eighteen-year-
old Michael Brown in Ferguson Missouri. According to
Black Lives Matter, police attempted to arrest Brown for
"jay-walking" and then shot him when his hands were in
the air and he was trying to surrender. "Hands Up Don't
Shoot" became a slogan of the movement—propagated
by the nation's leading media organizations. The slogan
and jay-walking claim were designed to demonstrate the
cold-blooded injustice of Brown's death. Both were lies.

As video from security cameras showed, Michael
Brown was a street thug who had just committed a
strong-arm robbery, brutalizing a much smaller Asian
shopkeeper in the process. When an officer tried to arrest
Brown for the robbery, the much larger Brown attacked
the officer and tried unsuccessfully to take his gun, injuring him in the process. Brown then charged the officer
while ignoring commands to stop. The officer shot Brown
in self-defense.[114]

The "Hands Up Don't Shoot" hoax was concocted by
Brown's accomplice in the strong-arm robbery. Six Black
eyewitnesses testified to the Grand Jury that, far from
having his hands up, Brown was charging the officer head
down when he was killed. The Obama Justice Department,
led by Black Attorney General Eric Holder, conducted a

---

114 https://www.nationalreview.com/2014/11/ferguson-fraud-rich-lowry/; https
    ://www.nationalreview.com/2019/08/elizabeth-warren-kamala-harris
    -ferguson-michael-brown/; https://www.breitbart.com/politics/2014/10/22
    /autopsy-michael-brown/

two-month special investigation that exonerated the officer. Yet nearly ten years later, Black Lives Matter was still
spreading the same lies through Netflix films and other
national media, while the criminal co-founder of Black
Lives Matter, Patrisse Khan-Cullors,[115] was given a contract with Warner Brothers TV to write a television series
in which she could peddle her inflammatory racial lies.[116]

The fictions propagated by Black Lives Matter in
the Brown case were typical of all the cases of alleged
racial injustice that Black Lives Matter used to organize
its insurrections.[117] These outbursts of violence caused
billions in property damage,[118] burned federal buildings
and police headquarters, and killed dozens of individuals
during the worst eruption of civic violence during peacetime in the nation's history. In the midst of the chaos and
the lawlessness, Black Lives Matter launched a "De-Fund
the Police" campaign which led directly to a record crime
wave in which thousands of mainly Black citizens were
killed by other Blacks.

The Democrat Party was entirely complicit in this
destructive mayhem. Led by Vice President Kamala
Harris, Democrats organized funds to bail out Black Lives
Matter criminals, accepted millions of Black Lives Matter

115 https://www.discoverthenetworks.org/individuals/patrisse-cullors/

116 https://variety.com/2020/tv/news/black-lives-matter-founder-patrisse-cullors
-warner-bros-television-group-overall-deal-1234806076/

117 David Horowitz, *I Can't Breathe: How A Racial Hoax Is Killing America*,
2021, pp. 61-147.

118 https://www.youtube.com/watch?v=Wp7hl2x2dDY&t=616s

donations to its political campaigns, tied the hands of local police through its control of major American cities, and laid the blame at the door of law enforcement agencies, calling them "systemically racist," even though they were more often than not under the control of Black police chiefs, mayors, and Democrats generally and innocent of the charges Black Lives Matter made against them.[119]

In August 2015, the Democratic National Committee passed a formal resolution endorsing Black Lives Matter's unfounded slanders against police: "The DNC joins with Americans across the country in affirming 'Black Lives Matter,' and the 'Say her name' efforts to make visible the pain of our fellow and sister Americans as they condemn extrajudicial killings of unarmed African American men, women and children." The Democrat statement, for which there was no evidence, went on to allege that "[The American Dream] is a nightmare for too many young people stripped of their dignity under the vestiges of slavery, Jim Crow, and White Supremacy."[120]

Democrat leaders' support for the incendiary lies and lethal crimes of Black Lives Matter were on full display when five officers protecting a Black Lives Matter demonstration in Dallas were assassinated by a Black racist named Micah Johnson. The assassinations occurred on July 7, 2016. It was the deadliest incident

---

119 https://www.the-sun.com/news/1520376/black-lives-matter-bail-criminals
       -kamala-harris/

120 https://www.buzzfeednews.com/article/darrensands/dnc-to-vote-on
       -resolution-supporting-black-lives-matter#.dk140ZjWA

for law-enforcement officers since the 9/11 attacks. The shooter, Micah Johnson, was interviewed for two hours by Dallas police chief David Brown, who was also Black. Johnson told Chief Brown that he "wanted to kill white people, especially white officers." Since the shooter was not about to surrender and was still armed and firing his weapon randomly, Brown gave the order to kill him.[121]

Black Lives Matter founder Patrisse Khan-Cullors replaced this reality with a characteristic fiction. Ignoring the fact that the killer was a homicidal maniac and the police chief who gave the order to kill him was Black, Khan-Cullors lamented the execution of the assassin, presenting it as a typical example of America's zeal to kill Blacks and treat them as less than human simply because they were Black. In her autobiography she described the shooter as "the first individual ever to be blown up by local law enforcement. They used a military-grade bomb against Micah Johnson and programmed a robot to deliver it to him. No jury, no trial. No patience like the patience shown the [white] killer who gunned down nine worshippers in Charleston, . . ."[122] Police negotiated with Johnson for two hours during which he never offered to surrender. The white racist shooter in Charleston did not resist arrest like Johnson but surrendered immediately.

---

121 Horowitz, op. cit., pp.112-113.

122 https://books.google.com/books?id=6l4mDwAAQBAJ&pg=PT11
&lpg=#v=onepage&q&f=false

President Obama responded to the tragedy by inviting Black Lives Matter leaders to the White House, where he praised them for "speaking truth to power." At the funeral for the murdered officers, with their widows and fatherless children in attendance, Obama laid the blame for the homicides squarely at the feet of the victims and their ancestors: "We also know that centuries of racial discrimination, of slavery, and subjugation, and Jim Crow; they didn't simply vanish with the law against segregation. . . . We know that bias remains."[123] Ignoring the racist malice and criminal destructiveness of Black Lives Matter, Obama praised their leaders, saying: "They are much better organizers than I was when I was their age, and I am confident that they are going to take America to new heights."[124]

On the campaign trail in 2020, Joe Biden repeated the now familiar Black Lives Matter lie that street thug Michael Brown was a victim of police racism. Biden then endorsed the malicious claim that "systemic racism" was at the root of the problem, in the form of police misconduct: "It's been six years since Michael Brown's life was taken in Ferguson—reigniting a movement. We must continue the work of tackling systemic racism and reforming policing."

---

123 Horowitz, op. cit., p. 116; https://www.breitbart.com/politics/2015/09/17 /valerie-jarrett-meets-black-lives-matter-leaders-white-house/; https://www .npr.org/sections/thetwo-way/2016/07/12/485713944/president-obama -speaks-at-dallas-memorial-service;

124 https://www.politico.com/story/2016/02/obama-civil-rights-meeting-219453

The full extent of Black Lives Matter's influence on the Democrats' agenda only became evident, however, when Joe Biden entered the White House as president-elect in November 2020. A letter from Black Lives Matter founder Patrisse Khan-Cullors was waiting for him: "Black people won this election," Cullors claimed. "Alongside Black-led organizations around the nation, Black Lives Matter invested heavily in this election. 'Vote and Organize' became our motto, and our electoral justice efforts reached more than 60 million voters. We want something for our vote. We want to be heard and our agenda to be prioritized."[125]

Addressing "President-Elect Biden and Vice President-Elect Harris" directly, Cullors then said: "Both of you discussed addressing systemic racism as central to your election campaigns. The best way to ensure that you remedy past missteps and work towards a more just future for Black people—and by extension all people—is to take your direction from Black grassroots organizers that have been engaged in this work for decades, with a legacy that spans back to the first arrival of enslaved Africans."[126]

Biden obliged. In his Inaugural address, January 20, 2021, he issued Executive Order 13985, which he introduced with these words: ". . . a historic movement for justice has highlighted the unbearable human costs of

125 https://blacklivesmatter.com/wp-content/uploads/2020/11/blm-letter-to
    -biden-harris-110720.pdf
126 Ibid.

systemic racism." Then he announced, "It is therefore the policy of my Administration that the Federal Government should pursue a comprehensive approach to advancing equity for all, including people of color and others who have been historically underserved, marginalized, and adversely affected by persistent poverty and inequality."[127]

Calling a movement that had incited a national lynch mob to destroy cities and accuse police of racial murders in advance of any investigation or trial "a historic movement for justice," did violence to both language and the facts. Describing the Black community, which had been the center of the nation's attention for fifty years since the passage of the Civil Rights Act, the beneficiary of trillions of dollars in government programs, of special race-based affirmative action privileges, and of the greatest social revolution in history—to call this community "underserved, marginalized and adversely affected by persistent poverty"—was a perverse attack on the country that had made America's Black population the richest, most privileged Black community in the world.

Days later, mining the same destructive vein, Biden made the following claim: "The fact is that systemic racism touches every facet of American life."[128] This was the clear implication of the Democrats' general libel that

127 https://www.whitehouse.gov/briefing-room/presidential-actions/2021/01/20
/executive-order-advancing-racial-equity-and-support-for-underserved
-communities-through-the-federal-government/

128 https://townhall.com/columnists/davidhorowitz/2021/10/05/black-lives
-matters-agenda-and-bidens-n2596597

America was a "white supremacist" nation. It was also a brazen lie. Neither Biden nor Black Lives Matter produced credible evidence for the claim that systemic racism was even a problem let alone one that touched every facet of American life. Moreover, the Civil Rights Act, which explicitly outlawed systemic racism, made such a claim completely implausible. If it were the case that systemic racism was pervasive in one or all of the eighteen thousand local police departments, for example, a tsunami of lawsuits would have been filed resulting in billions of dollars in legal damages. There was no such legal tsunami because "systemic racism" in twenty-first-century America was and remains a left-wing myth.

It was also the key myth that Democrats needed to promote their racist "Equity" agenda, which Biden included in an executive order at his inauguration. In the words of the order, "Our Nation deserves an ambitious whole-of-government equity agenda that matches the scale of the opportunities and challenges that we face."[129] Spelled out, this "equity" agenda was to use the power and wealth of the federal government to redistribute income and provide other benefits to every ethnic group except whites. This specifically included Asian Americans, like Vice President Harris, who constituted the richest ethnic group

---

129 https://www.whitehouse.gov/briefing-room/presidential-actions/2021/01/20 /executive-order-advancing-racial-equity-and-support-for-underserved -communities-through-the-federal-government/

in America, earning, per household, an average $20,000 more annually than whites.[130]

As a down payment on his "whole-of-government" equity agenda, Biden's first major legislation, a $1.9 trillion "American Rescue Plan Act," included $4 billion in "relief" to Black farmers—and Black farmers alone.[131] This was a program that had originated with Obama and was blatantly unconstitutional, as were all the Biden equity programs including those aimed at COVID relief, that were explicitly designed to help people on the basis of their skin color.

It was a repudiation of over two hundred years of sacrifice and struggle to create a color-blind, inclusive society. Yet it was the primary social agenda of the Democrat Party, which had chosen an incompetent woman to serve as Vice President because one of her parents—a Marxist professor—was a Black from Jamaica. The Biden White House also used a racial measure for numerous government appointments including one to fill a vacant Supreme Court seat. The new Supreme Court Justice, Ketanji Brown Jackson,[132] was a proponent of Critical Race Theory who regarded the Constitution she was appointed to defend a

130 https://www.financialsamurai.com/income-by-race-why-is-asian-income-so-high/

131 https://www.lawyerscommittee.org/5th-circuit-grants-intervention-to-black-farmers-to-defend-critical-usda-debt-relief-program/

132 https://www.discoverthenetworks.org/individuals/ketanji-onyika-brown-jackson/

"white supremacist" document which she was bound not to respect.

For all intents and purposes, the election of Joe Biden marked the potential end of the American experiment that had been launched by the founders and crowned by the sacrifices and heroisms of the civil rights movement and Martin Luther King Jr.

As if to symbolically confirm this end, only hours after his inauguration, Biden canceled the "1776 Commission," calling it "offensive" and "counter factual." The 1776 Commission was a project his predecessor had launched to restore respect for America's creation as a nation dedicated to the proposition that all men are created equal and endowed with a God-given right to liberty.[133] The 1776 Commission was a specific response to the attack on the founding by the 1619 Project,[134] whose false narrative of a nation born in slavery and still encumbered by its sinister influences was now formally embraced by the Biden administration and the political Left generally.

For the first time in American history, there was a government in Washington whose principles were fundamentally anti-American, and whose policies were self-consciously racist. Without dissent from Democrats

---

133 https://www.heritage.org/american-founders/commentary/bidens-disbanding -1776-commission-shows-lefts-war-us-history; https://www.whitehouse.gov /briefing-room/speeches-remarks/2021/01/26/remarks-by-president-biden-at -signing-of-an-executive-order-on-racial-equity/

134 https://www.discoverthenetworks.org/organizations/1619-project/

generally, the Biden administration had abandoned the egalitarian and pluralistic model inspired by Martin Luther, and secularized as America's constitutional framework by its Protestant founders and settlers two centuries earlier.

Part Three

The Tribe of Tyrannical Faiths

The attacks by the Left on America's liberal civic order have been fueled by the same tribalism that created the totalitarian regimes of the modern world—communism, fascism, and Nazism. To effectively combat these malignant forces, one must understand the relation between the articles of their faith and the liberating principles that guided Martin Luther and the Americans he inspired.

The corruptions of the Church that Luther rebelled against were rooted in the fact that it bestowed its religious authority on the Roman Empire. This marriage of the sacred and profane led inevitably to the oppressive hierarchies and corrupt practices that Luther came to despise and reject.

Luther's unique perspective began with the perception that the problems afflicting mankind do not come from the outside but from within. They are problems created by human weakness and desires, symbolized by Adam and Eve's choice to know evil in direct defiance of God's command.

In Luther's view, the commandment not to covet (which not coincidentally is the core socialist passion) by itself renders every mortal ineligible for salvation, because none of us can perfectly obey it. Consequently, if salvation is possible, it is only by a divine grace—by faith in a redeemer who is immortal, who can see into a human soul and summon the kind of mercy that leads to a judgment that is just. Christian theologians call this "Justification by Faith." Emulating this divine grace, imperfect as it must be, leads to respect for others— for flawed others—who struggle, as do we all, with the impossible task of each day and each hour living a virtuous life. Luther's community of faith is a community of the unworthy. It is why limits must be placed on governmental authority—that is, on the authority any one of us has over another.

We make the life judgments that determine our fates as ignorant equals. None of us—and certainly no representative of the political state—can make a just judgment on the sum of another's life. No one is above this law. No one has the authority to erase a life by forcing its subject to repudiate that life. In Luther's Christianity, salvation is a matter between an individual soul and its Creator.

This idea was dramatized by Shakespeare in a scene in which the ghost of Hamlet's murdered father reproves Hamlet for venting his rage at his mother's betrayal in marrying his father's brother and murderer. The ghost commands Hamlet to, "Leave her to heaven." For Hamlet can no more see into his mother's soul than he can discern what is roiling his. What is sacrosanct in each of us is our conscience, the daily navigator of life's challenges and falls. Only a divinity who can see into our souls has the position to judge us and decide our fate justly.

The political state exists to protect us from each other, not to force us to fit its mold, or forbid us to have unwanted thoughts. The state does not exist to appropriate the authority of the Creator. This is Luther's view and it is the religious basis for a democracy that supports individual freedom.

Luther's community is not only a community of equals, but one that is tolerant and inclusive of equally flawed others. Equal before the law. It is the ideal toward which our aspirations are drawn, and which America had nearly realized after two centuries of struggle, but is under ferocious attack from within.

America's liberal ideal was a gift from Luther and the Protestants who wrote the Constitution. Out of respect for each other's diverse faiths, the founders created a political order that was secular and plural, and adopted an attitude of humility when it came to themselves. They enshrined as the first pillar of their Bill of Rights, freedom of conscience, and insisted on its free expression as the guarantor of all other rights.

Those sacred rights are now under siege. The siege has been conducted by radicals whose own commitments are derived from a crypto religion whose assumptions and values are antithetical to those of Luther and the American founders.

Consider Luther's point of departure—Justification by Faith. The imperfection that is our birthright imposes a limit on the temporal authority that can be asserted over imperfect beings like ourselves. We can punish the guilty for injuries to others, but we cannot deny the dictates of their conscience or force them to think as we do. When we make our plans for a constitutional order, we do so out of an appreciation for the flawed nature of those in whom we vest authority, and those whom that authority is designed to rule. We expect them to have divergent views and understand that our own freedom to pursue happiness is secured by the respect we give to others and expect from them in return.

For radicals, the opposite is the case. They regard themselves as social redeemers, carriers of a faith that will transform human beings themselves. They regard humankind not as the source of evil but as good by nature—corrupted and oppressed by society. Luther navigated between an earthly community, eternally flawed, and a heavenly paradise, ruled by God. Radicals dream of a paradise on earth, created and ruled by them.

They earn the right to rule by becoming "socially conscious" or "woke." By having "progressive" views, they are empowered to alter social rules and institutions to achieve social justice. The transformation of the individuals who make up the progressive vanguard is achieved through good works—by challenging the alleged injustices that oppress. One can earn an earthly salvation by the good work of pursuing a virtuous life: by challenging the oppressive nature of the social institutions that are allegedly responsible for human corruption. The purification of individual lives in the strugge for a redeemed world creates the conditions under which such a world is possible. When enough individuals are converted to politically correct ideas, mankind will be liberated, and the world will become a place where justice prevails. This is what makes all world transforming progressives totalitarians: the idea that having the politically correct ideas on everything makes them the guardians of the enlightened and just future, and licensed to create it by any means necessary.

The earthly paradise that radicals seek exists in their enlightened imaginations and is achieved by persuading or coercing others to share their enlightened values and expectations. By raising "social consciousness," a revolutionary vanguard is forged. This vanguard will remove by all means necessary the social structures and ideas that allegedly make human beings selfish, bigoted, and unjust. The good works that pave the way to social justice begin with championing the values on which the earthly paradise depends. By correcting or suppressing the thoughts, opinions, and desires that society has corrupted into selfishness, greed, and bigotry, the progressive vanguard can create a new enlightened consciousness. This progressive consciousness becomes the foundation of a new "socially just" world.

The innate goodness of human beings is reflected in the "woke" opinions of the politically correct, who make up the revolutionary vanguard. They become an army, purged of racist, sexist, and classist opinions and attitudes. They carry the seeds of the new world within them.

Every member of the progressive vanguard must embrace and defend the virtuous ideas that make social justice possible. That is their role in the army of the saints. Those who oppose them are "reactionaries"—the party of Satan—bearers of "old world" ideas that lead to bigotry and oppression. It is the militant and uncompromising virtue of the vanguard that creates the very possibility of redemption. Progressive thoughts and actions are the good works that rectify social injustice, and lift the world from its fallen state, restoring the values of sharing, fairness, and justice that are humanity's true nature.

Therefore, there can be no freedom of conscience, no deviation from the party line, no politically incorrect thoughts, since an enlightened conscience must be created and secured if mankind is to enter the promised land. Being politically correct in every aspect of normal life, down to using the proper pronouns and having pure thoughts, is required for the revolution to succeed, for a new world to be created. To deviate, to entertain or profess politically incorrect thoughts, is to sabotage the very possibility of a new world.

Therefore, deviations from the party line—even minor ones—must be suppressed, cancelled. They cannot be left to breathe and multiply because they are the carriers of reactionary thoughts that are bearers of the old prejudices and values, therefore mortal threats to the "social consciousness" that is essential to the creation of a liberated future.

The religion that promises this social redemption is based on the presumption that a "socially just" world—paradise—is only possible if human beings are purged of society-imposed corruptions and able to maintain a politically correct outlook. This can only take place if the ideas and values of the old order are suppressed. The radical vision is a program of monolithic ideas and total control. It begins in the deceit that its promised land is one of equality and freedom. In fact, for all these reasons, the revolution is inevitably a tyranny with no limits and no exit.

Luther's gift is to have recognized and championed principles that are the foundations of liberty, tolerance, and democratic order. In a world where we are flawed in our nature and see through a glass darkly, individual conscience must be sacrosanct, a matter between God and His creation. If there is no God—a prospect that Luther did not consider—then a truly just judgment and correction of our lives is not possible. In this case, we are doomed to go on toiling in the imperfect and tragic circles that have defined our human passage from the beginning of time. But that is a far less dark prospect than a paradise with no air to breathe.

Appendix: A Radical Machiavelli

"We are five days away from fundamentally transforming the United States of America."
— Barack Obama

Conservative outlooks spring from observations about the past and are therefore as a rule pragmatic. Whatever "first principles" comprise such beliefs, they are (or should be) propositions that encapsulate the lessons of experience. Conservative principles are about limits, and what the respect for limits makes possible. By contrast, progressive views are built on expectations about the future. Progressive principles are based on ideas about a world that does not exist. For progressives, the future is not a maze of human uncertainties and unintended consequences, but a moral *choice*. To achieve "social justice" requires only that enough people will it.

This ambition leads to several unsavory consequences. First among them is an intolerance for beliefs that question its optimism. Such beliefs appear as obstacles to the progressive result, and therefore as both *reactionary* and immoral. Second, whereas conservatives defend ideals they believe have led to present good, the ideals progressives defend belong to a future that is only imagined. The significant impact of progressive attitudes lies in the negative stance they take towards the present reality. To annihilate this present is the practical goal of utopian desires. A fundamental aspect of the progressive aspiration is thus the disloyalty it inspires towards the actual communities its adherents inhabit. As the progressive philosopher Richard Rorty observed in a moment of candor: "You have to be loyal to a dream country, rather than one you wake up to every morning."[135]

By calling the progressive future a "dream country," Rorty underscored the dilemma confronting modern radicals who have given up trying to describe the society of the future with which they propose to replace the one they are bent on destroying. Marx scorned

---

135 Richard Rorty, *Achieving Our Future*, 1998. This aphorism was used as an epigraph in Michael Kazin's history of American leftism, aptly titled *American Dreamers*, 2011. Kazin's history is about the ideals he imagines leftists have contributed to America's heritage, not the actual actions leftists have conducted in the political arena.

nineteenth-century utopians because their ideas were based on wishful thinking. He regarded his version of socialism as "scientific" because its promised future was not a "dream country" but an inevitable outcome of the historical process. By the middle of the twentieth century, this Marxist illusion had become increasingly untenable; with the collapse of the Communist system its "science" became impossible even for progressives to credit. Consequently, they were faced with the dilemma of how to carry on a crusade that had led to such destructive consequences in the absence of a concrete plan to avoid them. The dilemma was resolved by an American radical named Saul Alinsky, whose influence eventually spread to so broad a spectrum of activists that it extended from former Weatherman radicals like Billy Ayers to his friend and political associate Barack Obama, and captured the heart of the Democratic Party itself.

By profession, Saul Alinsky was a "community organizer," but like everything else in his political life the term was a calculated camouflage for his real agenda, which was a world-transforming revolution (the original title of his most famous book was *Rules for Revoution*). Alinsky's preferred identification was "rebel" and his entire career was devoted to the destruction of America's social order, which he regarded as oppressive and unjust, and—in his words—worthy of "burning."[136]

---

136 *Rules for Radicals*, p. xiii.

Alinsky came of age in the 1930s, where he was drawn to the world of the gangsters he encountered while doing field studies as a graduate student in sociology at the University of Chicago. Alinsky sought out and became a social intimate of the Al Capone mob and its enforcer Frank Nitti, who became the gang's leader when Capone was sent to prison for tax evasion in 1931. Later, Alinsky said, "[Nitti] took me under his wing. I called him the Professor and I became his student."[137] While Alinsky was not unmindful of the fact that criminals were dangerous, as a good leftist he held "society"—and in particular capitalist society—responsible for creating them. In Alinsky's view criminality was not a character problem but a product of the social environment, and in particular the system of private property and individual rights, which radicals like him were determined to abolish.

Alinsky's career as an organizer spanned a period in which the Communist Party loomed as a major force on the American Left. Although he never joined the Party, his attitude towards Communists was fraternal, and he regarded them as political allies. In the 1969 "Afterword" to his book *Reveille for Radicals* he explained his attitude in these words: "Communism itself is irrelevant. The issue is whether they are on our side. . . ."[138] Alinsky's failure to oppose Communism extended to the Soviet regime. His biographer describes him as an "anti-anti Communist,"

---

137 Sanford Horwitt, *Let Them Call Me Rebel*, 1992, p. 20.
138 *Reveille for Radicals*, Vintage edition, 1969, p. 227.

and his attitude towards left-wing totalitarians contrasted dramatically with the extreme terms in which he was willing to condemn his own country.

A fraternal approach to the Communists was not universal on the Left at the time. In the 1930s, when Alinsky was starting out, Communists played a formative role in creating the CIO, the progressive coalition of industrial unions led by John L. Lewis and then Walter Reuther. But as the Cold War began, and the Red Army began toppling regimes in Eastern Europe, Reuther purged the Communists from the CIO. Reuther was a socialist but—unlike Alinsky—a militant anti-Communist and an American patriot. It is instructive that in *Rules for Radicals*, Alinsky, a deracinated Jew, refers to the exclusion of Communists, who were in practice Soviet agents, as a "Holocaust," a reference offensive to both Jews and to the inhabitants of America's democratic society. No Communist was sent to death camps in the McCarthy era, and only a handful of Communist leaders ever spent time in jail for their seditious activities and collaboration with America's enemies.

Like the generation of leftists that came of age after the Soviet collapse, Alinsky understood there were flaws in the Communist outlook. But like them, he never really examined what those flaws might be. He never questioned Marxism's fundamental view of society and human nature, or its goal of a socialist future, and never examined its connection to the epic crimes that Marxists committed. Alinsky never asked himself whether the vision of a society that was socially equal was itself the wellspring of the totalitarian state.

Instead, he identified the problem of Communism as one of inflexibility and "dogmatism," proposing as a solution that radicals should be "political relativists" and opportunists taking a flexible view of the means for achieving their ends. The revolutionary's task, as Alinsky saw it, was first to undermine the existing system and then see what happened (this was exactly Lenin's prescription). As a consequence, the guidelines Alinsky provided for activists were exclusively devoted to destroying the old order. No thought was given to ensuring that the result did not lead to totalitarian ends or greater oppression. He conceived the radical goal to be singular in purpose: to take power from the "Haves" so that it might be given to the "Have-nots." But he devoted no attention in his work to how a just redistribution might be accomplished without creating a totalitarian state.

Consequently, while his teaching might appear on the surface as "idealism," its prescriptions are deeply problematic. It is a declaration of war on a democracy whose individual freedoms are rooted in the institutions of private property, due process and limited government, all of which his prescriptions would destroy. Who is the "people," in whose name the revolution would act—and act without these constraints? History tells us that once the revolution is set in motion, "the people" is whomever the revolutionary elite designates, which is invariably itself.

To advance his political agendas, Alinsky created "community organizations," including a training institute for organizers called the "Industrial Areas Foundation." But his real influence came through his role as the Lenin of the post-Sixties Left. Alinsky's work became the practical guide for progressives who had supported Communist causes during the Cold War and were demoralized when the socialist fantasy collapsed, and who needed a theory that would enable them to regroup for a renewed assault on the capitalist foe.

Alinsky wove the inchoate theories of the post-Communist left into a coherent strategy of political organizing. His vision helped to forge the coalition of communists, anarchists, liberals, Democrats, Black racialists, and social justice activists who comprised the post-Cold War left. This left launched the "anti-globalization" movement just before 9/11, and the anti-Iraq War movement just after, and mobilized their forces to help elect one of their own to the White House in 2008; as it happens, a twenty-year Alinsky disciple. As Barack Obama put it at the height of his presidential campaign: "We are the ones we've been waiting for."[139]

Alinsky's political strategy contrasted with that of Sixties radicals who had advanced their revolution "in the streets," and rejected the Democratic Party as a Trojan Horse, which threatened to co-opt their agendas. They did not seek to infiltrate the institutions of American

---

139 http://www.youtube.com/watch?v=molWTfv8TYw

society and government. Tactically, they were confrontationalists. "Up Against the Wall" and "The Sky's the Limit" were their characteristic slogans, and mass protests their preferred form of action. By contrast, Alinsky urged radicals to infiltrate the Democratic Party and traditional institutions with the goal of subverting them. Rhetorical moderation was his stock in trade. While Tom Hayden and Abbie Hoffman were marching on Lyndon Johnson's Pentagon ("Hey, hey LBJ, how many kids did you kill today?") and fomenting riots at the Democratic convention, Alinsky's organizers were insinuating themselves into Lyndon Johnson's "War on Poverty" program, directing federal funds into their own organizations and causes and signing up as Democratic party activists.

The Sixties Left had no connection to the labor movement, but Alinsky did. The most important radical labor organizer of the time, United Farmworkers leader Cesar Chavez was trained by Alinsky, and worked for him for ten years. Alinsky's confrontations were not preparations to overthrow the state but were designed as bargaining chips to secure a bigger piece of the pie, and gain leverage for the next round. When racial unrest erupted in Rochester, New York, activists called on Alinsky to help them pressure Kodak to hire Blacks, a form of racial extortion that foreshadowed the direction of civil rights activism in the era of Jesse Jackson and Al Sharpton.

Alinsky also pioneered the alliance of radicals with the Democratic Party, which ended two decades of hostile conflict that climaxed in the convention riot of 1968. Alinsky was appalled by the riot. Radicals should not be warring against Democrats in the streets, he wrote, but organizing to become the delegates inside the convention hall.[140] Through Chavez, Alinsky had met Robert Kennedy (who supported his muscling of Kodak executives), who was one of the avenues through which Alinsky organizers made their way into the inner circles of the Democratic Party.

In 1969, the year that publishers reissued Alinsky's first book, *Reveille for Radicals*, a Wellesley undergraduate named Hillary Rodham (later to be known as Hillary Clinton) submitted a ninety-two-page research project on Alinsky for her senior thesis.[141] In her conclusion, Clinton compared Alinsky to Eugene Debs, Walt Whitman, and Martin Luther King Jr., as someone who was considered dangerous not because he was a self-declared enemy of the American system, but because he "embraced the most radical of political faiths—democracy."

The title of Clinton's thesis was "There Is Only the Fight: An Analysis of the Alinsky Model." In this title she had identified the single most important Alinsky contribution to the radical cause—his embrace of political nihilism. An SDS radical once wrote, "The issue is never the issue. The issue is always the revolution."[142] In other words, the cause of a political action—whether civil rights or women's rights—is never the real cause; women,

---

140 *Rules for Radicals,* p. xxiii.
141 http://www.msnbc.msn.com/id/17388372/
142 The statement appeared in *New Left Notes*.

Blacks, and other "victims" are only instruments in the larger cause, which is power. Battles over rights and other issues, according to Alinsky, should never be seen as more than occasions to advance the real agenda, which is the accumulation of power and resources in radical hands. *Power* is the all-consuming goal of Alinsky's politics.

This focus on power was illustrated by an anecdote recounted in a *New Republic* article that appeared during Obama's presidential campaign: "When Alinsky would ask new students why they wanted to organize, they would invariably respond with selfless bromides about wanting to help others. Alinsky would then scream back at them that there was a one-word answer: 'You want to organize for *power*!'[143] In *Rules for Radicals*, Alinsky wrote: "From the moment an organizer enters a community, he lives, dreams, eats, breathes, sleeps only one thing, and that is to build the mass power base of what he calls the army."[144] The issue is never the issue. The issue is always building the army. The issue is always the revolution.

Guided by these principles, Alinsky's disciples are misperceived as idealists; in fact, they are practiced Machiavellians. Their focus is invariably on means rather than ends. As a result they are not bound by organizational orthodoxies or theoretical dogmatisms in the way their still admired Marxist forebears were. Within the

---

143 Ryan Lizza, "The Agitator," *The New Republic*, 3/9/07. http://www .pickensdemocrats.org/info/TheAgitator_070319.htm. The source of the anecdote is Horwitt, op., cit.

144 *Rules for Radicals*, p. 113.

framework of their revolutionary agendas, they are flexible and opportunistic and will say anything (and pretend to be anything) to get what they want, which is power.

Communists identified their goal as a "dictatorship of the proletariat," which generated opposition to their plans. Alinsky and his followers organize their power bases without naming their goal, except to describe it in abstract terms like "social justice" and an "open society." They do not commit themselves to specific institutional aims whether it is the dictatorship of the proletariat or government ownership of the means of production. Instead, they focus on identifying their opponents as "Haves" and the "privileged," and work to build a power base to undermine the existing arrangements based on private property and individual liberty, which lead to social inequalities. By refusing to commit to principles or to identify goals they are better able to organize coalitions of the disaffected, which otherwise would be divided over the proper means to achieve their ends, and thus accumulate power.

The demagogic banner of Alinsky's revolution is "democracy," as Hillary Rodham observed. But it is not democracy as Americans understand it. Instead it is a radical democracy in which earned hierarchies based on achievement and merit are targeted for destruction. To Alinsky radicals, "democracy" means replacing all those who are in power with representatives of "the people." It is an old, discredited idea recast. Revolutionary elites mobilize the "oppressed" as a battering ram to bring down the system, and make their own way to power.

The democracy that Alinsky radicals intend is Leninist not Madisonian, a radical leveling of everyone but the revolutionary elite.

When Hillary Clinton graduated from Wellesley in 1969, she was offered a job at Alinsky's training institute in Chicago. She opted instead to enroll at Yale Law School, where she met her husband and future president, William Jefferson Clinton. In March 2007, the *Washington Post* reported that she had kept her connections to the Alinsky network even in the White House: "As first lady," the paper noted, "Clinton occasionally lent her name to projects endorsed by the Industrial Areas Foundation (IAF), the Alinsky group that had offered her a job in 1968."[145]

Unlike Clinton, Barack Obama never personally met Alinsky but as a young man became an adept practitioner of his political methods. In 1985, a group of twenty churches in Chicago offered Obama a job helping residents of poor, predominantly Black, South Side neighborhoods. The group was part of a network that included the Gamaliel Foundation, which operated on Alinsky principles. Obama became Director of the Developing Communities Project, an affiliate of Gamaliel, where he worked for the next three years on initiatives that ranged from job training to school reform to hazardous waste cleanup. A reporter who researched the projects sums

---

145 http://www.washingtonpost.com/wp-dyn/content/article/2007/03/24/AR2007032401152_pf.html

them up in these words: "the proposed solution to every problem on the South Side was a distribution of government funds . . ."[146]

Three of Obama's Chicago mentors were trained at the Alinsky Industrial Areas Foundation, and for several years Obama himself taught workshops on the Alinsky methods.[147] Beginning in the mid-1980s, Obama began work as legal counsel for the Alinsky organization, ACORN, soon to become the largest radical organization in the United States.[148] Gregory Galluzo, one of Obama's three Alinsky mentors, shared his training manual for new organizers with the *New Republic*'s Ryan Lizza, which he said was little different from the version he used to train Obama in the 1980s. According to Lizza, "It is filled with workshops and chapter headings on understanding power: 'power analysis,' 'elements of a power organization,' 'the path to power.' Galluzzo told me that many new trainees have an aversion to Alinsky's gritty approach because they come to organizing as idealists rather than realists. The Alinsky manual instructs them to get over these hang-ups. 'We are not virtuous by not wanting power,' it says. 'We are really cowards for not wanting power,' because 'power is good' and 'powerlessness is evil.'"[149] For Alinsky and his followers, power—a means—is in fact the end.

---

146 David Freddoso, *The Case Against Barack Obama*, 2008, cited in http ://www.discoverthenetworks.org/individualProfile.asp?indid=1511

147 Ryan Lizza, "The Agitator," *The New Republic*, 3/9/07.

148 http://www.discoverthenetworks.org/individualProfile.asp?indid=1511

149 Ibid.

According to Lizza, who interviewed Obama as well as Galluzzo, "the other fundamental lesson Obama was taught was Alinsky's maxim that self-interest is the only principle around which to organize people. (Galluzzo's manual goes so far as to advise trainees in block letters: get rid of do-gooders in your church and your organization.') Obama was a fan of Alinsky's realistic streak. 'The key to creating successful organizations was making sure people's self-interest was met,' he told me, 'and not just basing it on pie-in-the-sky idealism. So there were some basic principles that remained powerful then, and in fact I still believe in.'" On Barack Obama's presidential campaign website, one could see a photo of Obama in a classroom "teaching students Alinskyan methods. He stands in front of a Blackboard on which he has written, 'Power Analysis' and 'Relationships Built on Self-Interest, . . .'"[150]

In 1986, at the age of twenty-three and fresh out of Columbia University, Obama was hired by the Alinsky team "to organize residents on the South Side [of Chicago] while learning and applying Alinsky's philosophy of street-level democracy."[151] From that time until he became an elected legislator in 1996, the focus of his political activities was ACORN. A summary of his ACORN activities was compiled by the *Wall Street Journal*:

---

150 Ibid.

151 http://www.washingtonpost.com/wp-dyn/content/article/2007/03/24
    /AR2007032401152.html

In 1991, he took time off from his law firm to run a voter-registration drive for Project Vote, an ACORN partner that was soon fully absorbed under the Acorn umbrella. The drive registered 135,000 voters and was considered a major factor in the upset victory of Democrat Carol Moseley Braun over incumbent Democratic Senator Alan Dixon in the 1992 Democratic Senate primary. Mr. Obama's success made him a hot commodity on the community organizing circuit. He became a top trainer at Acorn's Chicago conferences. In 1995, he became ACORN's attorney, participating in a landmark case to force the state of Illinois to implement the federal Motor Voter Law. That law's loose voter registration requirements would later be exploited by ACORN employees in an effort to flood voter rolls with fake names. In 1996, Mr. Obama filled out a questionnaire listing key supporters for his campaign for the Illinois Senate. He put ACORN first (it was not an alphabetical list).[152]

After Obama became a US Senator, his wife, Michelle, told a reporter, "Barack is not a politician first and foremost. He's a community activist exploring the viability of politics to make change." Her husband commented: "I take that observation as a compliment."[153]

Alinksy dedicates his signature work, *Rules for Radicals,* to the devil, the first rebel: "Lest we forget,

152 http://online.wsj.com/article/SB10001424052970204488304574427041636
      360388.html#

153 Lizza, op., cit.

an over-the-shoulder acknowledgment to the very first radical: from all our legends, mythology, and history (and who is to know where mythology leaves off and history begins—or which is which), the first radical known to man who rebelled against the establishment and did it so effectively that he at least won his own kingdom—Lucifer."

Thus, at the very outset, Alinsky tells us what a radical is. He is not a reformer of the system, even God's system, but its would-be destroyer. In his own mind the radical is building his own kingdom of heaven on earth. But since a kingdom of heaven built by human beings is an impossible dream, the radical's real world efforts are directed to subverting and destroying the society he lives in. He is a nihilist. In *The 18ᵗʰ Brumaire* Marx summed up the radical passion by appropriating a comment made by Goethe's Mephistopheles: "Everything that exists deserves to perish."

Alinsky's tribute to Satan reminds us that the radical illusion is an ancient one and has not changed though the millennia. Recall how Satan tempted Adam and Eve to destroy their paradise by telling them that if they ate from the Tree of Knowledge they would be "as gods." This is the radical *hubris*: to create a new race of men and women who are able to live in harmony and according to the principles of social justice. To create such a race requires the total control—the totalitarian control—of individual behavior. Not incidentally, the kingdom the first radical "won," as Alinsky so thoughtlessly puts it, was *hell*. Typical of radicals not to notice the ruin they leave behind.

The book that follows the dedication to Lucifer begins with a friendly critique of the Sixties' New Left. What bothers Alinsky about Sixties radicals is their honesty. While the Old Left—American Communists—pretended to be Jeffersonian Democrats and "progressives," forming "popular fronts" with liberals and infiltrating the Democratic Party, New Left radicals disdained these deceptions, regarding them as a display of inauthenticity and weakness. To distinguish themselves from such popular front politics, Sixties radicals said to anyone who was listening that they were *revolutionaries* and proud of it.

New Left radicals despised liberals, staging riots at Democratic Party conventions. Slogans like "Up against the wall motherf—er" and "Off the Pig" telegraphed exactly how they felt about those who opposed them. Alinsky's chief advice to practitioners of what he regarded as infantile tactics is to *lie* to their opponents, instead—to disarm them by pretending to be moderates and liberals and willing to work with them. He complained about Sixties activists that they were "one moment reminiscent of the idealistic early Christians yet they also urge violence and cry, 'Burn the system down!' They have no illusions about the system, but plenty of illusions about the way to change our world. It is to this point that I have written this book."[154] In other words, the system—the American

---

154 *Rules for Radicals*, p. xiii.

system—should be burned to the ground, but to achieve this goal you must conceal your intentions. Conceal the goal and you can accomplish anything.

According to Alinsky, it is important for radicals to deal with the world as it is: "As an organizer I start from the world as it is, as it is, not as I would like it to be. That we accept the world as it is does not in any sense weaken our desire to change it into what we believe it should be— it is necessary to begin where the world is if we are going to change it to what we think it should be. That means working in the system."[155] It was with these Alinsky lines that Michelle Obama chose to sum up her husband's vision at the Democratic convention that nominated him for president. Referring to a visit he had made to Chicago neighborhoods, she said, "And Barack stood up that day, and he spoke words that have stayed with me ever since. He talked about 'the world as it is' and 'the world as it should be.' And he said that, all too often, we accept the distance between the two and we settle for the world as it is, even when it doesn't reflect our values and aspirations. But he reminded us that we also know what our world should look like. He said we know what fairness and justice and opportunity look like. And he urged us to believe in ourselves, to find the strength within ourselves to strive for the world as it should be. And isn't that the great American story?"[156] It was pitch-perfect Alinskyism.

---

155 *Rules for Radicals*, p. xix.

156 http://www.nytimes.com/2008/08/26/us/politics/26text-obama.html?ei=
	5124&en=48bdd187be31e21e&ex=1377489600&partner=permalink&expr
	od=permalink&pagewanted=print

As president, Barack Obama appointed Van Jones to be his "special assistant" for "green jobs," a key position in his plans for America's future. According to his account, Van Jones became a Communist during a prison term he served after being arrested during the 1992 Los Angeles race riots. For the next ten years, he was an activist in the Maoist organization STORM, whose acronym means "Stand Together to Organize a Revolutionary Movement." When STORM disintegrated, Jones joined the Apollo Alliance, an environmental coalition organized by Alinsky radicals, which subsequently played a major role in designing Obama's green programs. He also joined the Center for American Progress, a brain trust for the Democratic Party headed by John Podesta, former White House chief of staff in the Clinton Administration and co-chair of Obama's transition team.

In a 2005 interview, Van Jones explained to a reporter that he still considered himself a "revolutionary, but just a more effective one." "Before," he said, "we would fight anybody, any time. No concession was good enough; . . . Now, I put the issues and constituencies first. I'll work with anybody, I'll fight anybody if it will push our issues forward.... *I'm willing to forgo the cheap satisfaction of the radical pose for the deep satisfaction of radical ends.*"(emphasis added)[157] It was an embodiment of the Alinsky doctrine.

---

157 http://www.eastbayexpress.com/gyrobase/the_new_face_of_environmentalism
/Content?oid=290098&showFullText=true

"These rules," wrote Alinsky, "make the difference between being a realistic radical and being a rhetorical one who uses the tired old words and slogans, calls the police 'pig' or 'white fascist racist' or 'motherf—er and has so stereotyped himself that others react by saying, 'Oh, he's one of those, and then promptly turn off.'"[158] Instead, advance your radical goals by camouflaging them.

There is nothing new in the strategy of appearing moderate in order to disarm your opposition. It was Lenin's idea too, which is where Alinsky found it. Thus Alinsky turns to Lenin in the course of chiding rhetorical radicals of the Sixties over one of their favorite slogans (appropriated from the Chinese Communist dictator Mao Zedong). Comments Alinsky: "'Power comes out of the barrel of a gun' is an absurd rallying cry when the other side has all the guns. Lenin was a pragmatist; when he returned to what was then Petrograd from exile, he said that the Bolsheviks stood for getting power through the ballot but would reconsider after they got the guns."[159]

Lenin may have been a pragmatist, but only within the parameters of the revolution. He was a dogmatist in theory and a Machievellian practioner. He was always engaged in a total war, which he used to justify every means he thought might advance his goals. These included summary executions, concentration camps that

---

158 *Rules for Radicals*, p. xviii.
159 *Rules for Radicals*, p. 37.

provided a model for Hitler, and the physical "liquidation" of entire social classes. Lenin was the most dangerous kind of political fanatic—ready to resort to any means to get what he wanted, even if it meant pretending to be a democrat.

"[The] failure of many of our younger activists to understand the art of communication has been disastrous," Alinsky wrote. What he really meant was their *honesty* was disastrous—their failure to understand the art of *mis*-communication. This is the art he taught to radicals trying impose socialism on a country whose people understand that socialism destroys freedom: Don't sell it as socialism. Sell it as "progressivism," "economic democracy" and "social justice."

The very first chapter of Alinsky's manual for radicals, in which he proposes to set the framework for what follows, is called "The Purpose." Its epigraph is taken from the *Book of Job*: "The life of man upon earth is a warfare . . ." This is hardly an invitation to democratic politics, as understood by the American Founders. The American system was created to achieve compromise, and to bring warring factions into a working partnership. The Founders devised a system of checks and balances to temper popular passions and prevent them from cutting each other's throats.

In Alinsky's view the difference between the unethical behavior counseled by Machiavelli and the unethical behavior he would like to see practiced by radicals is merely that their political enemies are different. "*The Prince* was written by Machiavelli for the Haves on how to hold power. *Rules for Radicals* is written for the Have-Nots on how to take it away."[160]

Alinsky and his disciples view America's democracy as a hierarchical society similar to all those that went before it: "The setting for the drama of change has never varied. Mankind has been and is divided into the Haves, the Have-Nots, and Have-a-Little, Want Mores."[161] The claim is another Alinsky theft, in this case from the *Communist Manifesto*, which famously begins, "The history of all hitherto existing society is the history of class struggles" and then describes those struggles: "Freeman and slave, patrician and plebian, lord and serf, guild-master and journeyman, in a word, oppressor and oppressed, stood in constant opposition to one another, carried on an uninterrupted, now hidden, now open fight, a fight that each time ended, either in a revolutionary reconstitution of society at large, or in the common ruin of the contending classes."

This was nonsense when Marx wrote it—and worse, when one considers the tens of millions of individuals slaughtered by those who believed it. But it is the bedrock of radical belief, and the foundation of the left's destructive agendas. The idea that the world is divided into Haves and Have Nots, exploiters and exploited, oppressors and oppressed, leads directly to the conclusion that

---

160 *Rules for Radicals*, p. 3.
161 *Rules for Radicals*, p. 18.

liberation lies in the elimination of the former, which is the only way to end such a conflict. According to radicals, this will lead to the liberation of mankind. In fact, it led to the murders of 100 million people in the last century, and state-induced economic deprivation on a scale never witnessed before.

In the myth created by Marx, which all radicals to one degree or another believe, the market system is a zero sum gain where one man's gain is another's loss. Because the Haves will defend what is theirs, to achieve justice it is necessary to strip them of privilege and power. That is why radicals are organized for war—a stealth guerilla campaign at the outset, and a total war at the end. The myth of the Haves and the Have-Nots is a secular version of the religious vision of a world divided into Good and Evil. In addition to being followers of Machiavelli, Alinsky radicals are secular Manicheans. If it were true that all the social misery in the world were attributable to the greed and selfishness of one group, radicals would have a righteous case. But the claim is a fiction. Moreover, radicals acting on this claim have themselves have been the cause of the greatest human suffering on record.

Consider again the opening lines of the *Communist Manifesto*. The history of all previous societies is the history of "class struggle," of a war between the Haves and the Have Nots. Marx then names them through time. In Marx's schema, capitalists and business people are in our era the new oppressors, while proletarians—workers—are the new oppressed. Post-Communist radicals have added women, and racial minorities and even sexual minorities to the list of those oppressed, although to compare women and minorities in a democracy to slaves and serfs, and businessmen to slave-owners and feudal lords, is delusional and offensive.

But so are the categories "Haves" and "Have-Nots." There are tens of millions of capitalists in America, and they rise and fall with every economic wave. Where are the Enrons and Lehmans of yesteryear and where are their bosses? If proletarians can become capitalists and capitalists can become paupers, there is no class struggle in the sense that Marx and his acolytes claim, no system of oppression, no Haves and Have-Nots, and no need for revolution. The same is even more obviously the case where racial minorities and women are concerned. In the last decade America has had a Black president, two Black secretaries of state, three women secretaries of state, a chief law enforcement officer who is Black, and so forth, and so on. Many of the Fortune 500 companies are headed by women, some of them racial minorities. No slave or serf ever held such positions, or could. The radical creed is a religious myth. And a myth designed to provoke civil war.

In a democracy like America the notion that there are Haves and Have-Nots is akin to the Manichean view that the world is ruled by Satan and history is a struggle between the ruling forces of darkness and the liberating forces of light. In this radical vision, the "Haves" are

a category identical to "witches" in the Puritan faith—
agents of the devil—and serve the same purpose for the
preachers of this doctrine. The purpose is to identify one's
political enemies as instruments of evil and thus to justify
the total war against them.

Of course there is a partial truth in this malignant
vision, which is the only reason it is possible to sustain
it. There are *some* Haves, namely individuals who have
inherited wealth and merely have it, as opposed to those
who are active investors creating more wealth for themselves and others. There are also *some* Have-Nots, people
who were born to nothing and because of character flaws
or disabilities or other social dysfunctions have no way
of changing their circumstances. But it is false to describe
the economic divisions in American society in these terms,
or to imply that there are immovable social barriers to
individuals seeking to better themselves and increase their
wealth. If a person can move from one rung of the ladder
to the next, there is no hierarchy in Marx's sense and no
premise for revolutionary change.

In the real world of American democracy, social and
economic divisions are between the Cans and the Can-
Nots, the Dos and the Do-Nots, the Wills and the Will-
Nots. The vast majority of wealthy Americans, as a matter
of empirical fact, are first generation and have created and
earned what they possess. In the process of creating wealth
for themselves, they have created wealth for hundreds and
sometimes hundreds of thousands of others. But to describe
the wealthy as wealth *earners* and wealth *creators*, that is,

to describe them accurately, would explode the whole religious fantasy that gives meaning to radical lives.

Because the radical agenda is based on a religious myth, a reader of any radical text, including Alinsky's, will constantly come across statements that are patently absurd. According to Alinsky, "All societies discourage and penalize ideas and writings that threaten the status quo." The statement is again lifted directly from Marx, this time from his *German Ideology*, which claims that, "the ruling ideas are the ideas of the ruling class." From this false claim, Alinsky proceeds to the following preposterous conclusion: "It is understandable therefore, that the literature of a Have society is a veritable desert whenever we look for writings on social change." According to Alinsky this is particularly true of American society, which "has given us few words of advice, few suggestions on how to fertilize social change."[162]

On what planet did this man live and do his disciples now agitate to believe such stuff? How could they miss the narratives of "resistance" and "change," which have been familiar themes of our culture and dominant themes of our school curriculums, our presidency, and our political discourse? Alinsky's own book of advice on how to burn the system down is one of the most famous books of the time—recommended reading, in fact, on the official website of the National Education Association. But Alinsky presses on: "From the Haves, on the other hand,

---

162 *Rules for Radicals*, p. 7.

there has come an unceasing flood of literature justifying the status quo."

The reality is exactly the reverse. The curriculum of virtually every university department of Women's Studies, Black Studies, Peace Studies, Gay and Lesbian Studies, Asian, Chicano and Native American Studies, Cultural Studies, American Studies, and also anthroplogy, sociology, English, and Comparative Literature are openly dedicated to social change.[163] The goal of the most prestigious schools of Education, often incorporated into their formal mission statements, is "social change," and more specifically "social justice." (Bill Ayers has edited a series of instructional guides published by Columbia University on teaching social justice in the classroom.) Promoting social change and social justice have become routine subjects of commencement addresses, which are often given by anti-capitalist radicals such as Angela Davis, Michael Moore, and Bernadine Dohrn. The newest mass medium, the internet—features popular websites such as Daily Kos, MoveOn.org, and others too numerous to mention, which are dedicated to promoting the Alinsky program of taking wealth and power from the so-called Haves in the name of the so-called "Have-Nots." Finally there is the inconvenient fact that America's first Black president, a radical organizer and leader of an Alinsky organization himself, and a lifelong member of the political Left,

---

163 http://www.discoverthenetworks.org/viewSubCategory.asp?id=522
     #Curricular_Studies

announced on the eve of his election that "we are five days away from fundamentally transforming the United States of America."[164]

Alinsky's approach to political combat is captured in an anecdote provided by Alinsky's sympathetic biographer, Sanford Horwitt, in his book, *Let Them Call Me Rebel*. In this anecdote, Alinsky shared his wisdom with students wishing to protest the appearance on their campus of President George H. W. Bush, at the time America's representative to the UN during the Vietnam War:

> College student activists in the 1960s and 1970s sought out Alinsky for advice about tactics and strategy. On one such occasion in the spring of 1972 at Tulane University's annual week-long series of events featuring leading public figures, students asked Alinsky to help plan a protest of a scheduled speech by George Bush, then U.S. representative to the United Nations, a speech likely to be a defense of the Nixon Administration's Vietnam War policies [Note: the Nixon Administration was then negotiating with the North Vietnamese communists to arrive at a peace agreement—DH] The students told Alinsky that they were thinking about picketing or disrupting Bush's address. That's the wrong approach, he rejoined—not very creative and besides, causing a disruption might get them thrown out of school. [Not very likely—DH] He told them, instead, to go hear the speech dressed up as

---

164 http://www.youtube.com/watch?v=KrefKCaV8m4; cf. Stanley Kurtz, *Radical-in-Chief*, 2010 for a well documented account of Obama's leftist career.

members of the Ku Klux Klan, and whenever Bush said something in defense of the Vietnam War, they should cheer and wave placards, reading 'The K.K.K. supports Bush.' And that is what the students did with very successful, attention-getting results.[165]

This vignette illuminates Alinsky's ethics, and in particular his attitude towards means and ends. His model, Lenin, declared that the purpose of a political argument was not to refute one's opponent "but to wipe him from the face of the earth." In Lenin's mind his opponents were agents of evil and had to be destroyed. Alinsky's *modus operandi* is identical. It didn't matter to Alinsky that the Vietnam War was not a race war, or that millions of South Vietnamese opposed the Communists and welcomed the United States, or that the South was eventually conquered and occupied by North Vietnamese armies who turned the country into a prison. It didn't matter to Alinsky who George Bush actually was or what he believed. In a war, the objective is to destroy the enemy—by any means necessary.

Alinsky's recommendation to the student protesters was to take a symbol of one of the greater evils Americans had been associated with, and employ it with the intention of obliterating the memory of everything good America ever did. If America's cause in Vietnam was the Ku Klux Klan, then its cause was evil and America was evil. If George Bush was a spokesman for the Ku Klux Klan, no

---

165 *Let Them Call Me Rebel*, pp. xv-xvi.

more need be said. His destruction was not only justified, it was morally obligatory. In Alinsky's war, the real
individual, George Bush, is made to disappear so that the
enemy George Bush can be defeated. These are the methods of political argument that Lenin perfected and that
radicals have employed ever since.

Consequently, the most important chapter of Alinsky's
manual is titled "Means and Ends." It is designed to
address his biggest problem, which is how to explain to
idealistic radicals who think of themselves as creating
a world of perfect justice and harmony, that the means
that they must use to achieve that world are dishonest,
deceitful, and ruthless—and therefore indefensible by the
moral standards they claim to be upholding. The radical organizer has no such standards, Alinsky explains; he
"does not have a fixed truth—truth to him is relative and
changing; *everything* to him is relative and changing. He
is a political relativist."[166]

True liberals are not relativists. They may share the
radical's utopian agenda of a just and peaceful world but
they also have scruples. While they support radical ends,
their principles cause them to withhold their support when
radicals use means that may defeat the ends. It is because
they have scruples that Alinsky's contempt for liberals
is boundless. In his first book, *Reveille for Radicals* he
wrote: "While liberals are most adept at breaking their
own necks with their tongues, radicals are most adept at

---

166 *Rules for Radicals*, pp. 10-11.

breaking the necks of conservatives."[167] In contrast to liberals, who in Alinsky's eyes are constantly tripping over their principles, the rule for radicals is straightforward: the ends justify the means.

It is not because radicals begin by being unethical people that they approach politics this way. On the contrary, their passion for a future that is ethically perfect is what drives their political agendas and causes others to mistake them for idealists. But the very nature of this future—a world without poverty, without war, without racism, and without "sexism"—is so desirable, so noble, so perfect in contrast to everything that has preceded it as to justify any and every means to make it a reality.

If the radicals' utopia were actually possible, it would be criminal *not* to deceive, to lie, and to murder in order to advance the radical cause. If it were possible to provide every man, woman, and child in the world with food, shelter and clothing as a right, if it were possible to end bigotry and human conflict, what sacrifice would not be worth it, what crime not justified? The German philosopher Nietzsche had an epigram for this: "Idealism kills." The nobler the cause, the greater the crime it will justify. The great atrocities of the modern era, whether Nazi or Communist, were committed by idealists—people who believed they were saving mankind.

If the goal is to overthrow an existing social order, it is necessary to break its rules. Consequently, to be radical is

---

167 *Reveille for Radicals*, p. 21.

to be a willing outlaw. During the Sixties, SDS leader Tom Hayden once described the utility of the drug culture, while claiming he was not part of it. Once you get a middle class person to break the law, he said, they are on their way to becoming revolutionaries.[168] In the Sixties, radicals were generally proud of the idea that they were linked to criminals. Gangsters such as John Dillinger and films such as *The Wild Bunch* and *Bonnie and Clyde*, which celebrated American outlaws, were popular among them. Abbie Hoffman's *Steal This Book* was a manifesto of the creed. Obama friend and Weatherman leader Bernadine Dohrn's tribute to the murderer Charles Manson was its extreme expression. This romance with evil continues to be expressed in radicals' affinity for criminals and their causes at home and abroad, as it was in Alinsky's early attraction to Capone's enforcer Frank Nitti, not to mention his dedication to Lucifer.

The Stalinist historian Eric Hobsbawm gave this romance an academic veneer in a book he wrote about Sicilian criminals whom he described as "primitive rebels"—in short, revolutionaries *avant la lettre*. One of the chapters of *Primitive Rebels* is titled "Social Bandits," criminals whom Hobsbawm regarded as avatars of "social justice," their activity "little more than endemic peasant protest against oppression and poverty."[169] In this, Hobsbawm showed his contempt for poor people

---

168 The comment was made to the author personally.
169 *Primitive Rebels*, p.5, Google edition.

who are law abiding. According to Hobsbawm, the activity of the "mob" is "always directed against the rich," and therefore acceptable.[170] The French radical Pierre-Joseph Proudhon also gave license to radicals to steal and destroy by coining socialism's most famous epigraph: "Property is Theft." In reality, of course, it is socialism that is theft.

Alinsky's entire argument is framed as an effort to answer liberals who refuse to join the radical cause, saying, "I agree with your ends but not your means." To this Alinsky replies that the very question "Does the end justify the means?" is "meaningless." The real question according to Alinsky is "Does this particular end justify this particular means?"[171] But even this formulation is at bottom evasive, since radicals are in a permanent war and "The third rule of the ethics of means and ends is that in war the end justifies almost any means."[172]

The sum and substance of Alinsky's lecture about means and ends was originally published forty years earlier in a famous pamphlet by the Bolshevik leader, Leon Trotsky. In a pamphlet he called *Their Morals and Ours*, Trostky explained the revolutionary creed in the course of justifying the bloody crimes that Russia's Communists had already committed.[173] "Whoever does not care to return to Moses, Christ or Mohammed; whoever is not satisfied

---

170 *Primitive Rebels*, op., cit. p. 7.

171 *Rules for Radicals*, p. 24.

172 *Rules for Radicals*, p. 29.

173 http://www.marxists.org/archive/trotsky/1938/morals/morals.htm.

with eclectic hodge-podges must acknowledge that morality is a product of social development; that there is nothing invariable about it; that it serves social interests; that these interests are contradictory; that morality more than any other form of ideology has a class character." In other words, there is no such thing as morality; there are only class interests—the interests of the Haves versus the Have-Nots. Right for a revolutionary is that which serves the Have-Nots and their cause, however immoral it may seem by commonly accepted standards of right and wrong.

"Whenever we think about social change," Alinsky writes, "the question of means and ends arises. The man of action views the issue of means and ends in pragmatic and strategic terms. He has no other problem." In other words, like Trotsky, Alinsky's radical is not going to worry about the legality or morality of his actions, only their practical effects. If they are seen to advance the cause they are justified. "[The radical] asks of ends only whether they are achievable and worth the cost; of means, only whether they will work." But how is one to judge whether they work except by the final result—the creation of a perfect future? Doesn't such a course corrupt the cause and shape its outcome? In practice, Marxists killed 100 million people—in peacetime—justifying every step of their way by the nobility of the mission. Their victims were "enemies of the people" and therefore disposable. How to prevent such terrible outcomes except by observing a moral standard?

Alinsky answers the question about corrupt means this way: *everybody does it.* "To say that corrupt means corrupt the ends is to believe in the immaculate conception of ends and principles. The real arena is corrupt and bloody. Life is a corrupting process . . . he who fears corruption fears life." In this jaundiced view, there is no one who is not corrupt, who does not lie, cheat, steal, murder; it is all just business as usual. In which case there is no distinction to be made between tolerant democracies and totalitarian dictatorships. In pursuing a radical politics, Alinsky advises, "one does not always enjoy the luxury of a decision that is consistent both with one's individual conscience and the good of mankind. The choice must always be for the latter."[174] But who determines what is good for mankind? In Alinsky's universe there is only the revolutionary elite, and there is no higher court of appeal.

The Russian novelist Dostoevsky famously wrote that, "If God does not exist then everything is permitted." What he meant was that if human beings do not believe in a good that is outside themselves, they will act as gods and there will be nothing to restrain them. Alinsky is already there: "Action is for mass salvation and not for the individual's personal salvation. He who sacrifices the mass good for his personal salvation has a peculiar conception of 'personal salvation;' he doesn't care enough for people to be 'corrupted' for them."[175] In other words,

---

174 *Rules for Radicals*, p. 25.
175 Ibid.

the evil that radicals may do is already justified by the fact that they do it for the salvation of mankind—as defined by them.

Notice the scare quotes Alinsky puts around the verb "corrupted," a sign that he does not actually believe in moral corruption, because he does not believe in morality itself. His morality begins and ends with the radical cause. The sadistic dictator, Fidel Castro, one of Alinsky's radical heroes, summarized this principle in a famous formulation: "Within the revolution everything is possible; outside the revolution nothing is possible." The revolution—the radical cause—is the way, the truth, and the life.

Beginning with Rousseau and Marx and extending to our own day, revolutionaries have never articulated an actual plan of the future they promise. The utopians who tried to build communities that would institute "social justice" failed. They failed to build just communities, and even failed to build communities that were viable. Revolutionaries like Lenin and Alinsky, who are prepared to burn down existing civilizations and put their opponents to the wall, never have a plan. What they offer is a destructive rage against the worlds they inhabit and what they provide is an emotional symbol of the future they propose—in Marx's case "the kingdom of freedom," in Alinsky's "the open society." These seductive images are designed to sanction fraud, mayhem, and murder, all justified as necessary to gain passage to the promised land. But revolutionaries never spend a moment thinking about how to make an actual society function: how to keep people from injuring each other; how to motivate them to work; how to provide incentives to those who will actually create wealth.

What if there is no future that can actually fulfill the revolutionary aspiration? Then the means employed to get there are what *make* the revolutionary future. Each step of the way creates a new world—the only new world that human beings can create. What revolutionaries like Lenin and Alinsky offer is not salvation but chaos—a chaos designed to produce a totalitarian state.

The Roman general Scipio Africanus wept when his legions burned Carthage because in its flames he saw the future of his beloved Rome. The ancients did not view history as a progress, but as a series of cycles in which civilizations come into being, rise, and fall. In the biblical story, an angel with a flaming sword stands at the Gates of Eden, preventing God's wayward children from returning to the paradise they abandoned. The fall of Adam and Eve is a parable of the impossibility of an earthly bliss. And could it be otherwise if the world that so obviously needs repair, is a world that we ourselves have made? This is the religious view of the circumstances in which we find ourselves; and it is also the conservative view; and it is also mine.